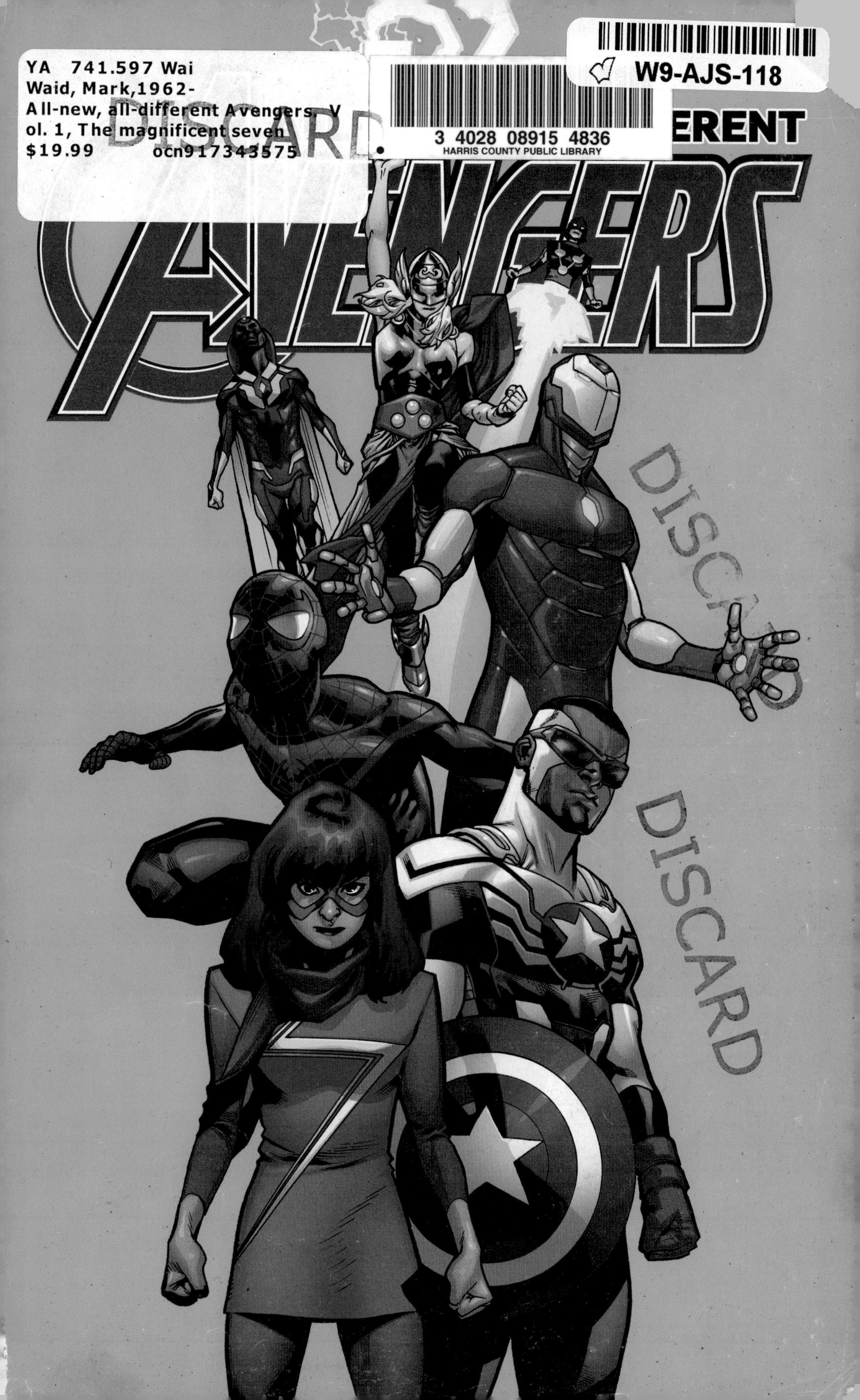
ALL-NEW, ALL-DIFFERENT
AVENGERS

ALL-NEW, ALL-DIFFERENT AVENGERS VOL. 1: THE MAGNIFICENT SEVEN. Contains material originally published in magazine form as ALL-NEW, ALL-DIFFERENT AVENGERS #1-6, AVENGERS #0 and FREE COMIC BOOK DAY 2015 (AVENGERS) #1. First printing 2016. ISBN# 978-0-7851-9967-0. Published by MARVEL WORLDWIDE, INC., a subsidiary of MARVEL ENTERTAINMENT, LLC. OFFICE OF PUBLICATION: 135 West 50th Street, New York, NY 10020. **Printed in the U.S.A.** ALAN FINE, President, Marvel Entertainment; DAN BUCKLEY, President, TV, Publishing & Brand Management; JOE QUESADA, Chief Creative Officer; TOM BREVOORT, SVP of Publishing; DAVID BOGART, SVP of Business Affairs & Operations, Publishing & Partnership; C.B. CEBULSKI, VP of Brand Management & Development, Asia; DAVID GABRIEL, SVP of Sales & Marketing, Publishing; JEFF YOUNGQUIST, VP of Production & Special Projects; DAN CARR, Executive Director of Publishing Technology; ALEX MORALES, Director of Publishing Operations; SUSAN CRESPI, Production Manager; STAN LEE, Chairman Emeritus. For information regarding advertising in Marvel Comics or on Marvel.com, please contact Vit DeBellis, Integrated Sales Manager, at vdebellis@marvel.com. For Marvel subscription inquiries, please call 888-511-5480. **Manufactured between 2/26/2016 and 4/4/2016 by R.R. DONNELLEY, INC., SALEM, VA, USA.**

10 9 8 7 6 5 4 3 2 1

ALL-NEW ALL-DIFFERENT

AVENGERS

THE MAGNIFICENT SEVEN

WRITER: MARK WAID

THE VISION & SCARLET WITCH IN
"EIDETIC"
(FROM *AVENGERS #0*)

ARTIST: MAHMUD ASRAR
COLOR ARTIST: SONIA OBACK

ALL-NEW, ALL-DIFFERENT
AVENGERS #1-3

ARTIST: ADAM KUBERT
COLOR ARTIST: SONIA OBACK
"YOU'RE A JERK" ARTIST: MAHMUD ASRAR
"YOU'RE A JERK" COLOR ARTIST: DAVE MCCAIG

ALL-NEW, ALL-DIFFERENT
AVENGERS #4-6

ARTIST: MAHMUD ASRAR
COLOR ARTIST: DAVE MCCAIG

LETTERER: VC'S CORY PETIT
COVER ART: ALEX ROSS

ASSISTANT EDITOR: ALANNA SMITH
EDITORS: TOM BREVOORT WITH WIL MOSS

+

FREE COMIC BOOK DAY 2015 (AVENGERS) #1

ARTIST: MAHMUD ASRAR
COLOR ARTIST: FRANK MARTIN
LETTERER: VC'S JOE SABINO

COVER ART: JEROME OPEÑA & FRANK MARTIN
ASSISTANT EDITOR: JON MOISAN
EDITORS: TOM BREVOORT WITH WIL MOSS

AVENGERS CREATED BY STAN LEE & JACK KIRBY

COLLECTION EDITOR: JENNIFER GRÜNWALD
ASSOCIATE EDITOR: SARAH BRUNSTAD
ASSOCIATE MANAGING EDITOR: ALEX STARBUCK
EDITOR, SPECIAL PROJECTS: MARK D. BEAZLEY

VP, PRODUCTION & SPECIAL PROJECTS: JEFF YOUNGQUIST
SVP PRINT, SALES & MARKETING: DAVID GABRIEL
BOOK DESIGNER: JAY BOWEN

EDITOR IN CHIEF: AXEL ALONSO
CHIEF CREATIVE OFFICER: JOE QUESADA
PUBLISHER: DAN BUCKLEY
EXECUTIVE PRODUCER: ALAN FINE

WHISPER HILL, MASSACHUSETTS.
--ALWAYS A LITTLE AWKWARD WHEN AN EX STOPS BY...
...WHAT? NO, THERE'S NOTHING "THERE." WE SIMPLY HAVE HISTORY, AND HE SAID HE NEEDS MY HELP WITH SOMETHING.
KNOK KNOK
I THINK I HEAR HIM NOW. CALL YOU LATER.
THE SCARLET WITCH.
I'M COOKING!
LET YOURSELF IN!
HELLO, WANDA.
OH, MY. SOMEONE'S PLUMBING THE OLD TIMES.

VISION? WHAT'S WRONG?
YOU LOOK UNSETTLED
IS EVERYTHING ALL RIGHT?
YOU LOOK LIKE YOU'VE SEEN A GHOST.
GHOST
GHOST
THIS IS WHY I WISHED TO SPEAK WITH YOU.
IT APPEARS THAT I AM BEING HAUNTED.

THAT'S AN...UNUSUAL STATEMENT COMING FROM A MAN WITH A COMPUTER MIND.
AS IT HAPPENS, I'M HERE AT WHISPER HILL TO ASSIST A DISASSOCIATED SPIRIT MYSELF...
...BUT LET'S GET YOU SQUARED AWAY FIRST.
HAVE A SEAT.
"A MECHANICAL MAN?" THOSE WERE THE FIRST CONVERSATIONAL WORDS YOU EVER SPOKE TO ME.
REALLY? FORGIVE ME. I DIDN'T MEAN FOR THEM TO BE HURTFUL.
YOU PATIENTLY LISTENED AS I EXPLAINED I WAS A SYNTHEZOID--IN ALL RESPECTS A HUMAN BEING, THOUGH CONSTRUCTED OF ARTIFICIAL MATERIALS.
YOU WERE WEARING BLUE AND SMELLED OF SASSAFRAS.
PERFECT MEMORY. TELL ME MORE ABOUT YOUR GHOSTS. WHEN DID YOU FIRST NOTICE THEM?
"TWELVE DAYS AGO. I WAS MAKING A FINAL PASS THROUGH AVENGERS TOWER. TONY STARK HAD SUGGESTED I RETRIEVE ANY PERSONAL EFFECTS BEFORE ITS SALE TO QENG ENTERPRISES.
"I ADMIT TO HAVING FELT QUITE MELANCHOLY. THE SENSE OF LOSS COUPLED WITH THE VACATING OF OUR HEADQUARTERS WAS STRONG. I BELIEVED MYSELF TO BE ALONE, BUT--"
VISION--

--YOU ARE NOW AN AVENGER!
WELCOME ABOARD, FRIEND!
HANK? T'CHALLA? CAP...?
YOU'RE YOUNG AGAIN? WHEN DID THIS--
?
"ILLUSIONS. GHOSTS. I WAS REMEMBERING-- RE-EXPERIENCING, IN THE MOST PRECISE DETAIL--THE DAY I WAS WELCOMED INTO THE AVENGERS' FOLD--
"--AS IF I'D STEPPED BACK IN TIME."
SO IT WAS... WHAT? A MEMORY MALFUNCTION?
QUITE THE OPPOSITE, IN FACT. BUT FOR CLARITY'S SAKE, ALLOW ME TO TELL THE STORY CHRONOLOGICALLY.
THE FREQUENCY OF SIMILAR APPARITIONS SWIFTLY ESCALATED.
"BEFORE LONG, EVERY OPEN FLAME REMINDED ME OF THE SHOCK OF LEARNING I WAS ORIGINALLY A HUMAN TORCH CREATED BY PHINEAS HORTON.
"EACH ASSEMBLAGE OF METAL VIOLENTLY RECALLED MY 'FATHER,' ULTRON.
"MY DAY-TO-DAY EXPERIENCES BECAME DANGEROUSLY UNTRUSTWORTHY. SELF-DIAGNOSTICS YIELDED NOTHING USEFUL. I FEARED I WAS GOING MAD.

"WITH NO CLUE AS TO WHAT WAS EFFECTING THIS STATE, YEARNING TO CLEAR MY CONSCIOUSNESS, I FLED NEW YORK IN SEARCH OF LESS...PROVOCATIVE SURROUNDINGS.
"EVENTUALLY, IT WAS IN RURAL ECUADOR THAT I RAN INTO THE MOST TELLING TROUBLE.
"A SMALL TOUR BUS HAD BEEN STRUCK BY A LANDSLIDE.
RRRRUMBLE
"TRAGICALLY, I WAS TOO LATE TO PREVENT THE HORROR. BODIES HAD ALREADY BEEN FLUNG FROM THE BUS, ALL DEAD.
"I HEARD ONE VOICE INSIDE, HOWEVER-- ONE SURVIVING VICTIM CRYING OUT FOR RESCUE."
"THAT'S AWFUL. BUT I'M SURE YOU KNEW JUST WHAT TO DO.
"IT'S THE KIND OF SITUATION YOU'VE DEALT WITH A HUNDRED TIMES BEFORE."

"EXACTLY.

"FOR IN THAT MOMENT, MY EARS WERE FILLED WITH THE SCREAMS OF EVERYONE WHO HAD EVER BEGGED ME FOR HELP.
"EVERY DESPERATE PLEA RECALLED WITH CRYSTAL CLARITY, DROWNING OUT THE ACTUAL VICTIM--ALL EQUALLY INSISTENT, EQUALLY VIVID.

"I HAD ONLY AN INSTANT TO CHOOSE--TO DISCERN THE REAL FROM THE IMAGINED--

"--AND GET THE TRUE VICTIM TO SAFETY."
NO...!
NO!

WHROOOM

YOU SAID IT YOURSELF EXACTLY SIX-AND-A-HALF MINUTES AGO:
I HAVE A PERFECT MEMORY.
AND IT'S BECOME TOO MUCH.
I CANNOT IMAGINE THE HORROR YOU'RE GOING THROUGH. EVERY EMOTION AUTOMATICALLY SPURRING A HURRICANE OF GHOSTLY RECOLLECTIONS...
WE... OF THE FLESH AND BLOOD VARIETY...WE HAVE THE LUXURY OF FORGETTING THINGS.
HOW COULD ANYONE FUNCTION IF EACH PAST WOUND, EACH BURIED TRAUMA, STAYED ETERNALLY FRESH...?
THE PAIN AND CONFUSION YOU MUST BE GOING THROUGH...HOW CAN I HELP?
YOU CANNOT.
THEN WHY DID YOU COME TO ME?
IN MY BRIEF LIFETIME, I HAVE HISTORICALLY CARED FOR YOU ABOVE ALL OTHERS. IT IS MY MEMORIES OF YOU THAT WERE MOST STRONGLY CODED TO MY EMOTIONS.
"WERE"...?
THEREFORE, YOUR PRESENCE IS THE ULTIMATE TEST.
WHAT?

"IT WAS EVIDENT THAT, WERE I TO STAY VIABLE AS A FUNCTIONING ORGANISM POSING NO RISK TO OTHERS, I HAD TO TAKE ACTION."
WHAT HAVE YOU DONE...?
I DO.
I DO.
"APPROXIMATELY AN HOUR AGO, I INTRODUCED INTO MY SYSTEM A SELF-CODED PURGING PROGRAM DESIGNED TO CORRECT THIS INTERNAL FAILURE."
VISION, STOP! TELL ME YOU'RE NOT ERASING YOUR MEMORIES...!
NO.

THE DANGER IS NOT WITH THE DATA I'VE STORED.
IT WAS IN THE FEELINGS THAT DRAW THE DATA INVOLUNTARILY FORTH.
...WHERE IS THE MAN I KNEW...?
WHAT HAVE YOU DONE...?
IT WAS THE EMOTIONS THAT HAD TO BE PURGED, WANDA MAXIMOFF.
WHAT HAVE YOU DONE?

1

YOU'RE A JERK!
AVENGERS ASSEMBLE.

12 HOURS EARLIER. NEW YORK CITY.
--LIVE AT THE QUEENSBORO BRIDGE, WHERE OUR NEWS VAN IS CAUGHT IN A MASSIVE PILEUP THAT--
--OH MY GOD--
--A CAR'S JUST BEEN PUSHED OFF THE BRIDGE BY A JACKKNIFING TRUCK--
--AND THERE ARE PEOPLE INSIDE!
HNNNNHH!

KSSSH
KSSSH
HANG ON!
HHNNNH!
C'MON... C'MON!
IS THAT--?
IT'S CAPTAIN AMERICA!
HNNFF!

GOOD CATCH, REDWING.
PHEW.
NOT MY CAPTAIN AMERICA...
DON'T BE A JERK, AUGIE.
AWESOME!
UPLOAD THAT! UPLOAD!
I GOT IT!
SHAKE HIS HAND!
CAPTAIN AMERICA! WILL YOU BUY OUR GIRL CADET COOKIES?
HEH.
SURE. I'M DOWN TO MY LAST FIVE BUCKS, BUT AFTER THAT I COULD DEFINITELY USE THE SUGAR...
...RUSH...
MINE!
NO, MINE!
GIRL CADET COOKIES
OOOH. THIS IS GOLD...
WHICH GIRL IS HE GONNA CHOOSE...?
PLACE YOUR BETS...

...
WAIT. IS THAT STARK?
NYU
LEND ME FIVE?
NYU
GIRL CADET COOKIES
GIRL CADET COOKIES
BETTER IDEA:
WHO WANTS THEIR PICTURE TAKEN WITH TONY STARK?
IRON MAN? WHOA!
YES, PLEASE!

INSTAPIC
@bigc
"THANKS" FOR THE "ASSIST."
I DIDN'T SEE THE ACCIDENT. I'M HERE IN TRAFFIC LIKE EVERYONE ELSE. OR DO YOU MEAN THE LACK OF CASH?
BECAUSE THERE'S NOTHING I ENJOY MORE THAN WATCHING YOU PRETEND TO LIKE CHILDREN.
ALSO, WHY'D YOU DRAG ME INTO THIS?
SMILE.
GIRL CADET COOKIES
SAVE
WAIT! YOU AIN'T STARK! WHERE'S YOUR ARMOR?
IN THE SHOP. HOP IN, CAP. I'LL GIVE YOU AND YOUR EAGLE A LIFT.
...MAN, DID HE GET LUCKY.
--WAS HE REALLY GONNA CHOOSE THE--
WELL, OF COURSE HE WOULD!
YOU'RE AN ASS.
GAME FACE, CAP.
REDWING'S A FALCON. YOU KNOW THIS.
AN EAGLE WOULD BE BETTER BRANDING. TELL HIM TO MIND THE UPHOLSTERY.

YOU HANDLED THAT WELL, BY THE WAY, SAM.
I TELL YA, THAT AIN'T--
THAT I HAD TO "HANDLE" IT AT ALL IS THE DRAINING PART. HAVING CAMERA PHONES AND CABLE NEWS AGENDA-IZING YOUR EVERY MOVE INTO A RACIALLY BASED NARRATIVE IS--
--IS--
--THE JOB. IT'S THE JOB.
A BIGGER PART THAN I'D LIKE, BUT I KNEW THE GIG WAS DANGEROUS WHEN I TOOK IT, RIGHT?
--STARK--
FROM THE MOMENT ROGERS HANDED IT OVER. YOU GUYS TALKING YET? AFTER THE BLOWUP YOU TWO HAD?
--OH, WOW.
NICE RIDE FOR A POOR MAN, THIS.
CASH POOR. YOU TRY SPENDING SIX MONTHS IN DEEP SPACE IN BETWEEN IRON MANNING, WATCH HOW METEORICALLY YOUR COMPANY CRATERS.

IF EVERY STARK DIME DOESN'T GO INTO REBUILDING, I MIGHT AS WELL START WORKING AT A GAS STATION.
OR, WORSE, PARKER INDUSTRIES.
HHGGH.
YOU HAD TO MAKE SOME GOOD BANK SELLING OFF THE TOWER.
"I DID OKAY. THE AVENGERS DIDN'T NEED IT."
"WAIT. AREN'T YOU AN AVENGER?"
"STEVE'S BARELY HAPPIER WITH ME THAN HE IS WITH YOU AT THE MOMENT. SUNSPOT HAS A GROUP CARRYING THE NAME, RIGHT?"
"NOT EXACTLY. AND ROGERS' TEAM IS ACTUALLY THE UNITY SQUAD. IT OCCURS TO ME, TONY...
S-12
"...I DON'T THINK THERE IS AN AVENGERS RIGHT NOW."
...THAT'S THE LAST OF STARK'S JUNK! AS THE NEW OWNER OF THIS SKYSCRAPER, I ORDER YOU TO MOVE IT OUT!

WAIT! WHATEVER THIS IS--YOU DID CYCLE IT DOWN?
WE CUT POWER TO EVERY COMPONENT! SOMETHING'S COMING IN FROM OUTSIDE--!
HOLY--
K-ZAAAK
Z-ZAKKAKK
GET BACK!
FCHOOM
FCHOOM
FCHOOM
FCHOOM
AIIEEE--!

<IT WORKED.>
<YOU HAVE ARRIVED ON SOL-3, WARBRINGER?>
<AS PLANNED. TELL THE RELAY TEAM THAT CELLULAR RECONSTITUTION WAS A SUCCESS.>
I'LL SAY IT WAS!
<THE NATIVE UNDERSTANDS ME? I'M NOT SPEAKING TERRAN-->
CLAP CLAP CLAP
I'M GOOD WITH LANGUAGES. CHITAURI, RIGHT? ONE HUNDRED NINETY-TWO WORDS FOR "HATE." YOU SHOULD BE ON TWITTER.
<SHUT UP.>

THAT IS A SMART METHOD OF TELEPORTATION, I HAVE TO SAY.
TRUST ME-- SOMEDAY, EVERYONE'S GOING TO REALIZE THAT IT'S MORE ENERGY EFFICIENT NOT TO BEAM MATTER, JUST INFORMATION, FOR ON-THE-SPOT CLONING AND THOUGHT TRANSFERENCE.
AND TO BE ABLE TO TARGET A LAB SUITING YOUR NEEDS FROM SUCH A DISTANCE--
SERIOUSLY, I'M A FAN.
<YOU'RE A FLEA. MY BUSINESS IS NOT WITH YOU.>
HEY! WHOA!
I DIDN'T SAY YOU COULD LEAVE.
?
<WHO-->
--WHO ARE YOU?
AN ALLY.
ESPECIALLY AGAINST NOVA.

AT THAT WHELP'S HANDS WHEN HE PUSHED YOU INTO THE SUN, NO?
"IT WAS IN ALL THE PAPERS."*
*AND IN NOVA #31. --TOM
I HAVE NO IDEA WHAT THAT MEANS, BUT I RECOGNIZE "SARCASM," THE LINGUISTIC TOOL EARTHLINGS ARE FAMOUS FOR. DO NOT MOCK ME.
IT'S AN ANACHRONISTIC PHRASE, ANYWAY. AND DON'T ASSUME WHERE I'M FROM.
DON'T ASSUME THIS IS EVEN MY TRUE FORM.
I REALIZE YOU'RE HERE TO SAVE FACE BY WREAKING HAVOC ON THIS PLANET FOR SPAWNING YOUR ATTACKER. YOU'LL BE THE TALK OF ALL THE CHITAURI. BUT--
--I PROMISE YOU, IF YOU TAKE ADVANTAGE OF THE OPPORTUNITY I'M OFFERING YOU, YOU'LL GO DOWN IN HISTORY AS A GALACTIC LEGEND.
AS THE WARLORD WHO ANNIHILATED THE HUMAN RACE.
YOU'RE NOT THE FIRST CHITAURAN TO VISIT EARTH. MILLENNIA AGO, ONE OF YOUR ANCESTORS LEFT AN ARTIFACT BEHIND--
--BROKEN INTO THREE PIECES, LEST IT BE DISCOVERED--

--FOR HERE IS WHAT IT CAN ACCOMPLISH. BEHOLD...
...WHAT ASSEMBLING THEM WILL DO TO THIS PLANET.
!
UH-OH.
TCH-TCH.
SOMEONE'S EAVESDROPPING.
SORRY TO INTERRUPT.
I JUST SWUNG BY--
--TO USE THE LITTLE BOYS' ROOM. IS IT FREE?

THOOM
...DON'T BLACK OUT, SPIDEY...SAVE THE *INNOCENT*...
...NO REST FOR THE WICKED...

...NNNNNNHH...
THWIP
NO!
THAP

GO LIMP.
I'VE GOT YOU.
THAP
HEY, LOOK! IT'S TRADEMARK-INFRINGEMENT KID! I KNOW YOU!
GOOD. DON'T BOTHER LOOKING FOR TONY STARK, THOUGH.

YOU WANT TO TELL ME WHY I HAD TO DOUBLE ACK BECAUSE YOU UST BLEW UP WHAT USED TO BE MY BUILDING?
I'M USUALLY MUCH BETTER AT THIS...
...AND THAT WASN'T... WASN'T ME...! I SWEAR!
I WAS JUST SWINGING BY WHEN I SAW AN ELECTRICAL FLARE! I WENT TO CHECK IT OUT AND--
--ALIEN! BIG, ANGRY ALIEN!
WELL, THAT'S DIFFERENT, THEN. YOU OKAY TO MEET ME BACK IN THERE?
YES, SIR.
TAK

LOOK FOR
IRON MAN.
HEADED OUT.
YOU CAN TAKE IT FROM HERE. I HAVE FAITH IN YOU. I'LL BE IN TOUCH.
SOMEBODY LOSE A SPIDER-KID IN HERE?
IF YOU'RE LOOKING FOR A FIGHT, PAL, LET ME SHOW YOU HOW IT'S DONE.
FIRST RULE OF COMBAT: DISARM THE ENEMY.

SECOND RULE: SURROUND AND CONQUER.
WAIT. IS IT HOT IN HERE OR IS IT JUST M--

SSSKOWWWWW
=SIGH=

THIS IS GOING TO BE EASIER THAN I *THOUGHT.*

BEFORE THE SUN SETS--
--THIS WORLD WILL BELONG TO ME!

!
!
SO THE QUESTION CAME UP: IF AND WHEN THEY EVER RE-ASSEMBLE, WHO'D BE A GOOD DRAFT FOR THE AVENGERS?
BRUNO HAS THE STRONGER OPINIONS.
NAKIA HAS THE LOUDER VOICE.
AND MY TERROR OVER ACCIDENTALLY COMPROMISING MY SECRET IDENTITY IS FORCING ME TO NOT DROWN THEM BOTH OUT IN A SEA OF EDUCATED OPINIONS.
IT'S KILLING ME.
SIX WEEKS AGO.
AT THE JERSEY CITY CIRCLE Q.

KAMALA, YOU ARE UNCHARACTERISTICALLY SILENT. WHO DO YOU THINK WOULD BE A GOOD AVEN--
CAPTAIN MARVEL.
SHOCKED-I'M-SHOCKED. OF COURSE YOU'D PICK CAPTAIN MARVEL. SHE'S YOUR FAAAAVORITE.
SHUT UP SHUT UP SHUT UPPPP.
BRUNO KNOWS MY SECRET, AND HE L-O-V-E-S TO GET IN-JOKEY IN FRONT OF OUR OTHER FRIENDS SOMETIMES.
LATER, I WILL SHRINK DOWN AND PUNCH HIM IN THE EARDRUM.
REGARDLESS... CAN WE ALL AGREE NO WOLVERINE?
WHAT DO YOU HAVE AGAINST WOLVERINE? SHE'S AWESOME!
STEALTHY...SKULKY... MUCH HOTTER THAN THE OLD WOLVERINE WAS...
THOOM
!
WHAT WAS THAT?
NO WAY. IT'S...IT'S...

...IT'S A NIGHTMARE!
BEEN FOLLOWING A BAND OF BEASTS ALL THE WAY FROM ARIZONA TO THE EAST COAST TODAY. MAN, THE LEAPS ON THIS ONE...
LEAVE IT TO ME TO SAVE THE WORST FOR LAST.
CIRCLE
YO! UP HERE! LEAVE THE BYSTANDERS ALONE!
LIKE HE'S LISTENING. I ONCE HAD A DOG I COULDN'T HOUSEBREAK, AND HE LOVED ME.

BRUNO, WE HAVE TO GET OUT OF HERE!
I'M THE MANAGER! I GO DOWN WITH MY Q-SHIP!
NOT ME! MY PARENTS WILL BE FREAKING OUT ABOUT THEIR LITTLE BETI! I'M GOING HOME!
EVENTUALLY.
HEADS UP!
COMIN' THROUGH!
HEY, NICE LOOK.
NOVA?
HEY, MAYBE HE SHOULD HAVE BEEN IN MY DRAFT PICKS.
AAAAH!
CHILL! YOU'RE GOOD!
DESPITE APPEARANCES, I HAVE THIS TOTALLY UNDER CONTROL!

ONE BLAST FROM THIS, AND WHAT THE HELL--?
THIS IS...MY TURF... MONSTRO!
I DON'T APPPRECIATE...THE INTRUSION...!
WHOA.
I THINK I'M IN LOVE.
WITH THE GIRL.
THAT'S MS. MARVEL.

I CAN'T FIRE WITH HER IN THE WAY, SO, INSTEAD, THIS:

THWAM
LOOK OUT! IT'S THE HUMAN ROCKET!

EEUURGH!

OKAY, SO THAT WAS A LITTLE SHOW-OFFY, BUT IT WORKED. SHE'S WIDE-EYED.

WAS THAT NECESSARY?
HAH?
YOU PUNCHED THE TEETH OUT OF AN INNOCENT CREATURE--
--AND YOU SLAMMED HIM NEARLY THROUGH A DRY CLEANERS THAT'S BEEN IN THIS NEIGHBORHOOD FOR GENERATIONS!
I HOPE THEY HAVE DUMB BEAST INSURANCE--
--NOTHING PERSONAL!
OW. TOO FAR, KAMALA, BUT...
...MAN, NOBODY TOLD ME NOVA WAS A FLYING JACKHAMMER!
GHAH. RECOVER! SAY SOMETHING NICE, SAM!
WOW, YOU'RE REALLY HUGE.
D'OH.
I WASN'T BORN THIS SIZE. BESIDES, IT'S NOT A BUG, IT'S A FEATURE. I CALL IT "EMBIGGENING."
THERE. A VACANT LOT WE CAN FIGHT IN, AT LEAST. WHERE'D THIS THING COME FROM?
AN ATOM IN ARIZONA.
"A CRAZY ALIEN UNLEASHED HIGH-JUMPING MONSTERS FROM THE MICROVERSE.
"I'VE BEEN ROUNDING THEM UP ALL DAY. ALL I HAVE TO DO IS RE-SHRINK THIS ONE, PREFERABLY BEFORE IT JUMPS INTO MANHATTAN--
"--WHICH I CAN DO IF YOU'LL PLEASE STOP DANCING WITH IT!"

AAAUGH. THAT WAS SUPPOSED TO SOUND LIKE A JOKE, SAM, NOT AN ORDER.
WOW. HE SURE LIKES GIVING ORDERS.

YOU. YOU HAVE CRUSHED YOUR LAST TOYOTA.
'BYE.

AND SCENE. TO THE MICROVERSE HE RETURNS.
I'M SURE THAT'S A COMFORT TO THE DRY CLEANERS.

NNNH. TOO HARSH. HE DID MEAN WELL. WHAT IS WRONG WITH ME? HE DIDN'T DESERVE THAT...DID HE?

GREAT. SHE THINKS I'M A LUNATIC. DON'T BE NERVOUS. JUST SAY SOMETHING FUNNY. SAY SOMETHING FUNNY.
SO...

...YOU WANT TO GO FLATTEN A COFFEEHOUSE OR SOMETHING...?
WHAT?
NO!
NO! I SAID FUNNY!

WAIT--!
GOTTAGOBYE.

UGH. I HATE HOW TWITCHY AND TONGUE-TIED I GET AROUND OTHER SUPER HEROES WHEN I MEET THEM. EVEN THE ARROGANT ONES.
I WISH I COULD JUST RELAX. I SOUNDED LIKE A COMPLETE--
HEY.
AAAAAH!
SORRY! SORRY! I--I DIDN'T KNOW YOU WERE--I WAS JUST--
ARE YOU STALKING ME?
NO! OH, WOW, NO!
OH, NO! MY JACKET! DOES HE RECOGNIZE IT? DOES HE REMEMBER MY FACE?
REVERSE TIME. REVERSE TIME!
=KAFF=
OR DOES HE JUST NOT UNDERSTAND THAT IT'S NOT COOL TO SNEAK UP ON WOMEN IN ALLEYWAYS?
WHY ISN'T HE SAYING ANYTHING?
YOU DIDN'T MEAN TO SNEAK UP ON HER. SHE'S REALLY NICE, AND NOW YOU'VE FREAKED HER OUT.
YOU'VE GOT, LIKE, ONE LAST CHANCE TO FIX THIS, BUCKETHEAD. SO DO SOMETHING DRASTIC TO MAKE PEACE.
SOMETHING DRAMATIC.

LET'S START OVER.
MY NAME IS SAM.
OH, GOD.
...
OH, GOD.
WHAT...IS HE... DOING...?
WHAT THE HELL IS HE DOING PUTTING ME ON THE SPOT LIKE THIS?
DOES HE NOT GET THAT I HAVE GOOD REASONS FOR KEEPING MY NAME SECRET? IS HE EXPECTING ME TO TAKE MY MASK OFF?
SHOULD I TAKE MY MASK OFF?
I BARELY KNOW HIM! I MEAN, I DIDN'T TELL HIM TO UNMASK! HE JUST DID IT!
LOOK AT HIM. HE THINKS HE'S BEING SWEET. MAYBE HE IS, I DON'T KNOW! I FEEL LIKE I OUGHT TO SAY OR DO SOMETHING, BUT...I...I...

...I DIDN'T ASK.

WAIT! SAM, I--
IT'S NOT "SAM."
WHAT?

...
I JUST SAID THAT. I CAN'T BELIEVE YOU FELL FOR IT.
WHAT?

WHY DID I LIE? HOW WAS THAT A RECOVERY? THERE'S NO COMING BACK FROM THAT!
SCREW IT. LET THIS DAY BE OVER. THE GOOD NEWS IS WE'LL NEVER HAVE TO CROSS PATHS AGAIN.
I CAN'T BELIEVE...!
GOD, I ALMOST WARMED UP TO THAT CHOWDERHEAD!
WHERE'S HE FROM, AGAIN? ARIZONA? GOOD!
IF I NEVER SEE HIM AGAIN, IT WILL BE TOO SOON.
"YOU'RE A JERK!"

2

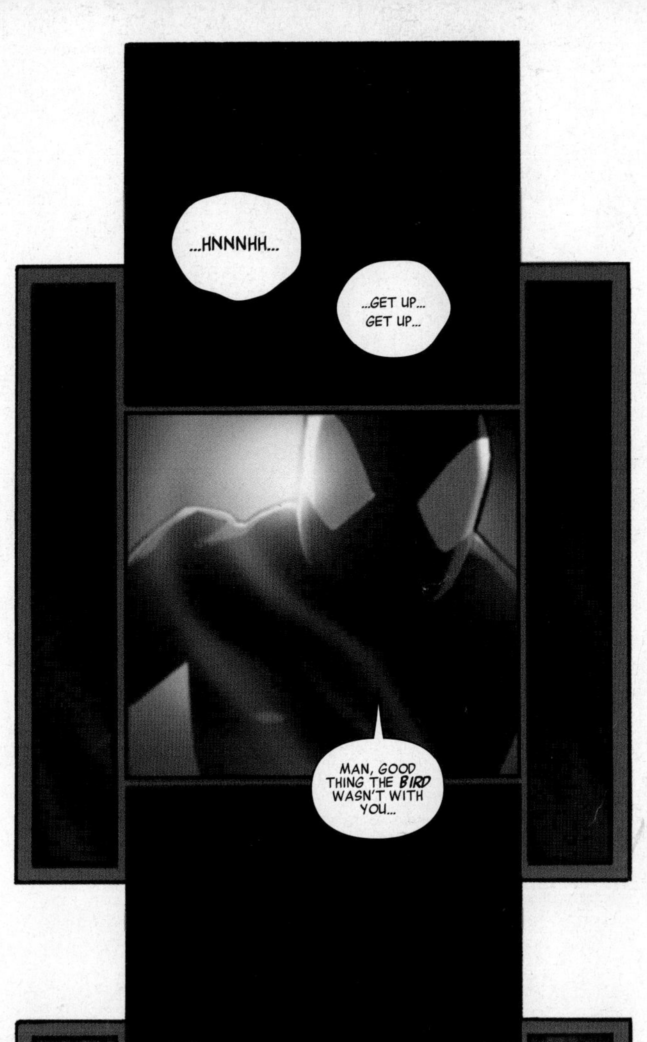
...HNNNHH...
...GET UP... GET UP...
MAN, GOOD THING THE BIRD WASN'T WITH YOU...

!
...SPIDER-MAN...?
PRETTY MUCH. DON'T MOVE. I'VE WEBBED OVER YOUR WOUNDS, BUT THEY'RE GONNA NEED SOME TREATMENT. THAT'S WHAT I COULD DO FOR YOU--
THWIPP
THWIPP
THWIPP
--BUT I DON'T EVEN KNOW WHERE TO START WITH IRON MAN!

I MAY BE OF SOME ASSISTANCE.
THAT'S THE VISION RIGHT?
COOL.

MY SENSORY ALERTS ARE STILL ATTUNED TO THE ALARMS IN THIS TOWER, AS THERE IS STILL MUCH TO RETRIEVE.
I REGRET THAT I DID NOT ARRIVE IN TIME TO CONFRONT WHOEVER ATTACKED YOU--
--BUT IF I HURRY, I MAY BE ABLE TO INTERFACE MY OPERATING SYSTEM WITH STARK'S BEFORE HIS ARMOR TERMINALLY MALFUNCTIONS.
THERE! HIDDEN IN THE SUB-ENCRYPTION--AN EMERGENCY PROTOCOL I CAN OVERRIDE--
SPLANG
--TO SERVE AS AN AUTO-DISMANTLE!
GHHUHH!
THANK YOU. THE WHOLE SUIT WAS FLASH-MELTED IN AN INSTANT. IT WAS TOTALLY SEALED--
--AS I FOOLISHLY BELIEVED THIS FACILITY TO BE.

THIS TOWER ISN'T AN AVENGERS PLAYGROUND ANYMORE, STARK! IT'S MY PRIVATE PROPERTY!
IF YOU WANTED ONE LAST LOOK AROUND, YOU SHOULD HAVE MADE AN APPOINTMENT WITH MY OFFICE!
VISION, CAP...THIS IS MR GRYPHON, WHO PURCHASED THIS BUILDING FROM ME WHEN I NEEDED TO UNLOAD IT.
AND THIS IS, WHAT, SELLER'S REMORSE? REVENGE?
WHO'S PAYING FOR THIS DAMAGE?
ALL WE REALLY KNOW ABOUT HIM IS THAT HE'S AN UNPLEASANT MAN.
WHO'S THE SHORT ONE, AGAIN?
SPIDER-MAN.
WHAT, IS HE FRANCHISING NOW?
HE'S GOT THE OLDER SPIDER-MAN'S SEAL OF APPROVAL. MAYBE EVEN MINE.
ABOUT THE SKYSCRAPER, MR. GRYPHON...IT'S AVENGERS POLICY TO COVER PROPERTY...
...DAMAGE...
...EXCEPT WE'RE NOT THE AVENGERS ANYMORE AND TONY HAS NO...
...EHHH.
FROM THE SHADOWS, I SAW SOMEONE WITH THE ALIEN, BUT I CAN'T SEEM TO REMEMBER HIS FACE OR VOICE. THAT'S WEIRD.
DID YOUR SPIDER-SENSE NOT KICK IN ON THE ALIEN'S SOLAR POWERS?
YEAH, TOO LATE.
WHAT ELSE YOU GOT?
VENOM BLAST. ALSO, CAMOUFLAGE. VERY USEFUL.
YET NEITHER OF WHICH CAN HELP US PINPOINT THE DIRECTION HE WENT.
YOU CANNOT GIVE CHASE WITHOUT ARMOR, TONY.
RELAX. THAT SUIT? JUST A ONE-OFF. TEMP STUFF.
STARK
"EVEN AS WE SPEAK, I'M UBERING THE CURRENT MODEL-PRIME FROM THE ENGINEERING LAB."

LADIES AND GENTLEMEN, THE CAPTAIN IS MAKING HIS FINAL APPROACH INTO NEWARK AIRPORT.
WE APPRECIATE YOUR PATIENCE GIVEN THE FLIGHT DELAY, BUT WE ARE DOING OUR BEST TO GET YOU TO THE GATE AS FAST AS HUMANLY--
ZOOM
--POSSIBLE--
IT CAN'T BE WARBRINGER. CANNOT.
I THREW HIM INTO THE SUN. DID HE SURVIVE THAT? DO CHITAURANS DO THAT? DOES HE WANT REVENGE?
THAT'S DUMB, SAM. YOU LIVE IN ARIZONA, NOT NEW YORK. IF IT WERE WARBRINGER, HE'D COME LOOKING FOR YOU, NOT VICE-VERSA.
(SO, WORLD HISTORY CLASS THAT I BAILED ON, BE GRATEFUL FOR THAT.)
SAM ALEXANDER!
FLU GOING AROUND GONNA BE SICK SORRY--!
12
NY BULLETIN ALERT: ALIEN INVADER PHOTOED IN NY, NJ

NY BULLETIN ALERT: ATTACK ON LIBERTY SCIENCE CENTER
NO, NO, NO, NO, NO...
NOT JERSEY CITY. PLEASE, NOT JERSEY CITY.
THAT'S HER TURF...!
LIBERTY SCIENCE CENTER
LACKWITS. THEY'RE MAKING THIS EASY FOR ME.
THE OTHER CHITAURAN FRAGMENTS I MAY HAVE TO UNEARTH. THIS ONE, HOWEVER...
...THIS ONE IS IN PLAIN SIGHT.
HEY!
CIRCA 12 A.D.
ARTIFACT OF UNKNOWN ORIGIN
DISCOVERED DURING
MUSEUM CONSTRUCTI

WHOEVER YOU ARE--
--WHERE DO YOU GET OFF TERRORIZING INNOCENT PEOPLE?
MS. MARVEL!
ANOTHER COLORFUL FLEA.
THIS PLANET IS POSITIVELY RIFE WITH VERMIN.
SHKOWW
WHOA!

GO! RUN!
THIS IS NOT THE TIME OR PLACE FOR CAMERAPHONES! GO MAKE A CAT VIDEO SOMEWHERE! GO!
KSSSH
OKAY. LOOKS LIKE YOU GOT WHATEVER YOU CAME FOR.
LET'S MOVE THIS NEXT PART TO A NICE, DESERTED LOT SOMEWHERE SO WE DON'T DESTROY THIS BEAUTIFUL--
THOOM
--BUILDING.

CRAP. IT IS WARBRINGER.
I'M NOT SURE WHO I'M MORE AFRAID OF HERE.
LET'S TAKE IT OUTSIDE, UGLY!
ARE YOU KIDDING ME?
I MEANT HIM, NOT YOU!
FWOOM
GHAAAH!
I KICKED YOUR CAN BEFORE, WARBRINGER. I CAN DO IT AGAIN.
THAT WAS A LIFETIME AGO, EARTHSKIN.
I'M NOT THE WEAKLING YOU REMEMBER.
AAAAAHH!
WILL YOU BACK OFF?

WHATEVER YOU STOLE, JUST HAND IT OVER AND WE'LL GO FROM THERE BEFORE YOU WRECK THE WHOLE BLOCK!
YOU SEEM TO CARE SO VERY MUCH FOR PROPERTY. IS THAT SPECIFIC TO ANTIQUES--
FWOOM
CHOOM
--OR IS IT JUST ANYTHING?
FWAASH

THE PEOPLE.
THERE ARE PEOPLE IN THOSE BUILDINGS...!
HEY, BUCKETHEAD! YOU STARTED THIS! HELP ME PUT OUT THE FIRE!

I DID NOT START--
OH, FOR THE LOVE OF GOD. DO WE HAVE EVERYONE OUT?
YEAH!

THEN I'VE GOT THIS!

STAND BACK!
FA-THOOOM!
SHRAKOOM
THAT...THAT BUILDING WAS SOMEONE'S LIVELIHOOD. IT'S BEEN HERE FOR DECADES...!
CONTAINED THE BLAZE.
YOU'RE A JERK!
EVERY TIME YOU COME HERE, YOU DESTROY THINGS!
I'M SORRY! PRIORITIES, OKAY? IT WAS EITHER DO DEMOLITION WORK OR WATCH THE FIRE SPREAD--!
LIKE YOU REALLY THOUGHT ABOUT THAT FOR A SECOND! THIS IS NOT ANGRY BIRDS! THINK ABOUT THE COLLATERAL DAMAGE!
THIS IS WHERE GOOD PEOPLE LIVE! WHERE BYSTANDERS ARE CLOSE!

THE ALIEN DOESN'T CARE! LET'S GET AFTER HIM! I'LL FLY YOU!
I'LL WALK.
!
YOU TWO ALL RIGHT?
I SEE YOU MET OUR PLAYMATE.
HOMINA.
YOU'RE... THE AVENGERS...
WE'RE NOT ACTUALLY THE AVENGERS ANYMORE, BUT I APPRECIATE YOUR VOTE OF CONFIDENCE.
HE'S CHITAURI. HE CALLS HIMSELF WARBRINGER.
HAVE YOU RUN INTO HIM BEFORE?
I--
"HEY, EVERYBODY, TURNS OUT WARBRINGER'S DESTROYING THINGS BECAUSE HE WANTS REVENGE ON NOVA. LET'S DROP BOTH OF THEM IN THE SUN."
SAY SOMETHING, SAM...
I SAW HIM FIRST, ACTUALLY.

I WAS SWINGING BY EX-AVENGERS TOWER WHEN I SAW A BUNCH OF ENERGY BUSTING OUT, AND I WENT TO INVESTIGATE.
THAT'S OKAY, RIGHT?
THAT'S FINE. DID HE INDICATE HIS PURPOSE IN ANY WAY?
HE STOLE AN ARTIFACT FROM THE MUSEUM. IT DIDN'T LOOK USEFUL.
HE'S TRYING TO COLLECT THREE OF THEM. WE CAN'T LET HIM. SOMEHOW HE TELEPORTED HERE BY KILLING PEOPLE AND STEALING THEIR MASS. IF HE FINDS ALL THREE, HE'LL--
--WELL, I DIDN'T QUITE GET THAT PART. BUT I'M PRETTY SURE IT'LL BE BAD.
THEN LET'S BEAT SOME ANSWERS OUT OF HIM. HE'S AT THE PATH STATION ON GROVE.
--ALL UNITS PROCEED TO THE AREA--
LOWLY WORMS.
THE CARBON SLUDGE YOU'RE MADE OF IS OF SUCH LOW QUALITY THAT I REQUIRE REPEATED DOSES TO HOLD THIS BODY TOGETHER...
...FOR NOW.
GROVE
ZZZZK

THWIPP
THWIPP
OH, NO YOU DON'T! NOT AGAIN!
I COULDN'T STOP YOU LAST TIME, BUT NOW I'M PUTTING YOU ON A DIET!
GUYS-WHO-SAY-THEY'RE-NOT-THE-AVENGERS, ASSEMBLE!
CLEAR THE AREA! WE'LL DO THE HEAVY LIFTING!
I'LL ASK YOU ONCE, WARBRINGER! WHAT DO YOU WANT?
IMMORTALITY.

TO LIVE FOREVER IN THE ANNALS OF HISTORY!

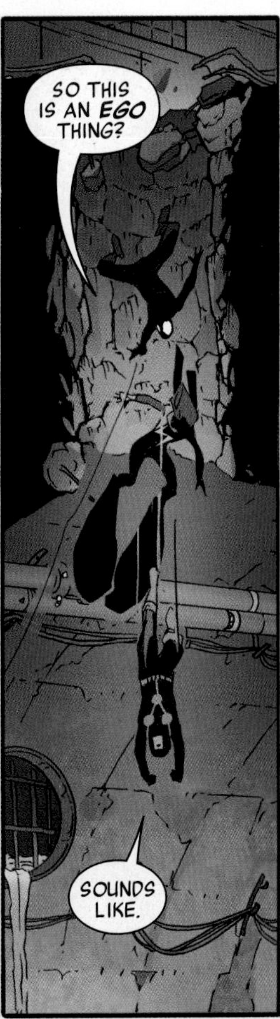
SO THIS IS AN EGO THING?
SOUNDS LIKE.

DO YOUR WORST.
YOU ARE EARTHLINGS.

YOU ARE NOTHING!

YOU ARE A DISMISSABLE INFESTATION ON A MINEABLE PLANET WITH RESOURCES VALUABLE TO THE CHITAURAN EMPIRE!

THWAM
NEVERTHELESS, THE TALE OF YOUR EXTINCTION AT MY HANDS--
--WILL BE TOLD THROUGHOUT THE MILLENNIA!
BEFORE MY DAY IS DONE, I SHALL SEE THE NAME WARBRINGER CARVED ACROSS THE CHITAURAN SKY IN LIGHTNING!
I THINK NOT, BRIGAND!
RRMMBBLL

NOT WHILE THE LIGHTNING IS MINE TO COMMAND.
THE MIGHTY THOR?

INTERESTING...
THOR, BE CAREFUL!
WATER'S EVERYWHERE! YOU SHOCK HIM, YOU SHOCK US!
NO MATTER. THUNDERBOLTS ARE BUT ONE OF MY WEAPONS!
FLY, MJOLNIR!

THOOM
OH
MY
SHORTS!
FAREWELL, INSECTS. REMEMBER MY NAME--

YOU CAN."

3

"THE TUNNEL BELOW FLOODED INSTANTLY. IRON MAN, THOR AND I SAVED THE REST OF YOU FROM BEING CRUSHED IN THE CURRENT...
"...AFTER WHICH THOR QUICKLY BEGAN CARDIOPULMONARY RESUSCITATION AS NECESSARY..."
PIZZA
...A CURIOUS EXPERTISE FOR THE GOD OF THUNDER TO HOLD.
EVEN IN ASGARD, PEOPLE DROWN, VISION.
YOU WERE CAUGHT BY SURPRISE, SAM. IT'S OKAY.
MY HELMET SHOULD HAVE PROTECTED ME--
HANG ON. YOUR NAME REALLY IS SAM?
YOU LIED TO ME?*
AW, JEEZ...
*ISSUE ONE. --TOM
HEY! HEY! WHATEVER THIS IS, WE DON'T HAVE TIME FOR HIGH SCHOOL DRAMA, OKAY?
WARBRINGER'S CLEARLY A TRAINED KILLER AND A WALKING VOLCANO, NOT A TEACHABLE MOMENT.
TAKE A KNEE. LET THE GROWN-UPS HANDLE THIS.
NO!

ADULTS DON'T GET THEIR WAY BY YELLING.
THAT HAS NOT NECESSARILY BEEN MY EXPERIENCE, CAPTAIN.
I LIKED YOU BETTER BEFORE YOU GAVE YOURSELF AN EMOTION-DECTOMY, VISION. YOU WERE LONGER ON COMMON SENSE.
JUST SAYING, CAP--
--TAIN-- SIR--
YOU, I'LL LISTEN TO.
KOFF
THE MORE OF US, THE SAFER EVERYONE WILL BE--CIVILIANS ESPECIALLY.
WE'RE JUST TAKING RESPONSIBILITY.
WELL.
CAN'T ASK FOR MORE THAN THAT.
C'MON. I'M SICK OF GETTING LED AROUND BY THE NOSE.
LET'S GO FINISH THIS.

HART ISLAND,
LONG ISLAND SOUND.

IT'S **HERE**, EARTHLING GRYPHON, ISN'T IT? THE **THIRD** AND **FINAL ARTIFACT**.
THE OTHER FRAGMENTS PULL TOWARDS IT LIKE **MAGNETS.**

CONGRATULATIONS, WARBRINGER. YOU ARE A **CREDIT** TO THE PROUD **CHITAURI RACE--**
--AND **FAR** BETTER AT HEAVY LIFTING THAN **I** AM.

YOU'VE **DONE** IT. YOUR NAME WILL BE TAUGHT TO **CHITAURAN SCHOOLCHILDREN.**
SKOW

"FORGET THE EXPERIMENTAL TECHNOLOGY THAT BROUGHT YOU HERE. ASSEMBLE THESE ARTIFACTS AS YOUR ANCESTORS INTENDED--
"--AND YOU WILL HAVE AT YOUR COMMAND, POURING THROUGH A VAST INTERSTELLAR PORTAL THAT IS PREPARING TO OPEN AS WE SPEAK, A MASSIVE ARMY OF RAVENOUS CHITAURI MARAUDERS--

"--EAGER TO ASSIST YOU
IN CLEANSING THIS DREADFUL
LITTLE MUDBALL OF LIFE!"

WELL DONE, GRYPHON.
WE'LL SAVE YOU FOR LAST. MY REWARD TO YOU.
I HAVE A DIFFERENT GIFT IN MIND. THEY'RE A LITTLE TOO VOLATILE FOR ME TO CONTROL NOW, BUT I NEED THE ARTIFACTS ONCE THE GATE'S OPEN.
BESIDES, YOU MAY NEED MY HELP EXPLAINING THE MISSION TO YOUR TROOPS-TO-BE.
"PUZZLING.
"THESE SOLDIERS. CHITAURI, YES-- BUT THEY WEAR NOT MY UNIFORM, NOR WIELD ANY WEAPON WITH WHICH I AM FAMILIAR."
YES. ABOUT THAT.
WE'LL DISCUSS IT AFTER.
AFTER WHAT?

TODAY'S SCIENCE LESSON:
TEMPERATURE ON THE SURFACE OF THE SUN? 6000 KELVINS.
TEMPERATURE OF LIGHTNING?
"FIVE TIMES THAT."
KRAKOOM

THWAM
THOOM
DO THESE FIT TOGETHER SOMEHOW?
YES--
NO! YES, THEY DO, BUT A DOWN-AND-DIRTY E.M. ANALYSIS FROM MY ARMOR SUGGESTS TO ME--
--THAT ASSEMBLY IS WHAT UNLOCKS THE WINDOW UP THERE!
"SO DON'T TOUCH THEM! WARBRINGER'S ON THE ROPES! WE'LL FIGURE OUT WHAT TO DO WITH THESE THINGS AFTER--"

NYYYAAAH--!
FRY.
THWAM
THWAK
OH, CRAP.
HE WAS FAKING. AND HE'S POWERFUL ENOUGH TO BAT THOR AND NOVA AROUND WHILE HE MELTS THE VISION.
NEW PLAN:
WE OPEN THE PORTAL.
EXCUSE ME?

UNLESS ONE OF YOU IS PACKING A GODPUNCH OR SOMETHING.
BUT THE ARMY--
--WON'T HAVE A CHANCE TO SPILL OUT--NOT IF WE TIME THIS TO THE MICROSECOND!
WHEN I GIVE THE SIGNAL, I NEED SPIDER-MAN TO COMBINE THE ARTIFACTS--
--THEN DESTROY THEM WITHIN A SPLIT-INSTANT!
WHY ME?
PROPORTIONATE SPEED OF A SPIDER, RIGHT?
RIGHT.
COMPLICATION, HOWEVER.
WHAT?
WHAT IS IT?
THE GRAVES!

NEVER MIND! JUST HANDLE IT! WORLD KINDA DEPENDS ON YOUR UNDIVIDED ATTENTION!
GO! GO! GO!
SPIDEY, BE READY!
DAAAH!
EASY FOR HIM TO SAY--!
HOW IS THIS HAPPENING?
SSSSS
NNNNHH!
SPIDEY, ON ZERO! FIVE--

--FOUR--
THEY'RE CLAWING AT THE ARTIFACTS!
...SEIZE IT...SEIZE IT...
UNHAND ME!
--THREEEEAARGH!
IRON MAN-- WE HAVE TO DO THIS NOW!
--JUST-- NEED A BREATH--
NO TIME! HURRY!

IMPETUOUS YOUNGLING! HE CANNOT--
NOVAAAA!
HE'LL MAKE IT, ALL RIGHT? HE HAS TO! SPIDEY, IT'S THREE--
NOT-- AGAIN--!
I-- WILL--DEFEAT-- YOU!
EARTH'S ANNIHILATION-- WILL BE--ON YOUR HEAD--!
--TWO--
FAT CHANCE!
--ONE--

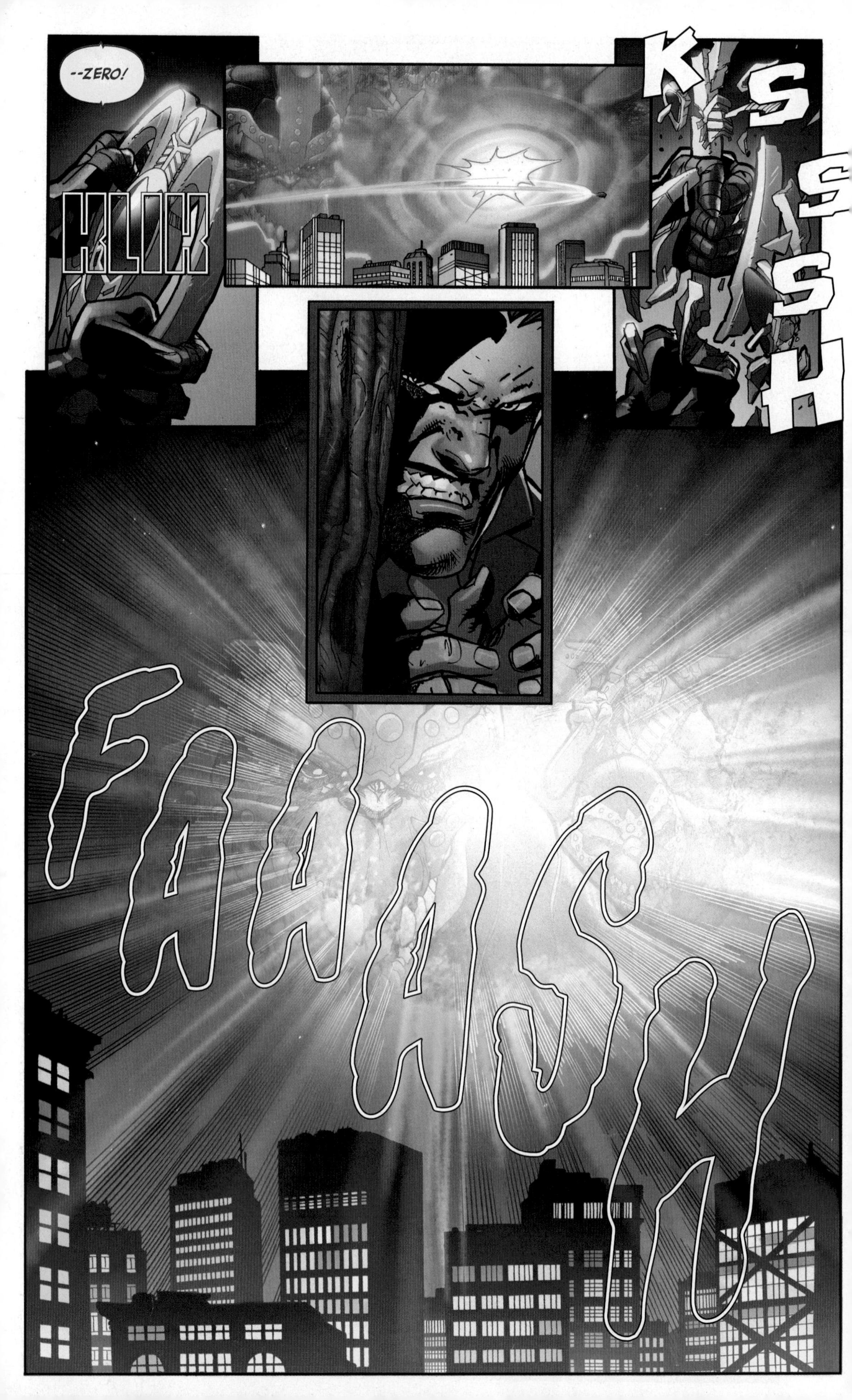
--ZERO!
KLIK
KSSSH
FAAASH

I REPEAT: DAAAAH.
WHERE'D THE ZOMBIES GO?
A SIDE EFFECT OF THE ARTIFACTS, MAYBE?
LET'S JUST SAY YES SO I DON'T HAVE TO THINK ABOUT IT.
MISSION ACCOMPLISHED. NICE GOING, YOU THREE.
WARBRINGER'S GONE. I STILL DON'T KNOW WHAT BROUGHT HIM HERE, BUT IF I NEVER HEAR THE WORD "EARTHLINGS" AGAIN, IT'LL BE TOO SOON.
HE SPOKE LIKE A WARLORD WITH A VENDETTA, BUT HE KNEW US NOT.
UNLESS... DID HE NOT CALL YOU BY NAME?
=SIGH=
HE... HE DID. BECAUSE-- BECAUSE--
BECAUSE ALL MEMBERS OF THE SPACEFARING NOVA CORPS ARE THUS ADDRESSED.
I WOULD IMAGINE A FIGURE AS AGGRESSIVE AS WARBRINGER HAS HAD MANY ENCOUNTERS WITH THE CORPS... WOULDN'T YOU?
I...WOULD IMAGINE.
YEAH.

SO... THAT'S IT, THEN...
NOT QUITE.
CAP SAID SOMETHING EARLIER THAT GOT ME THINKING.
ABOUT HOW NO ONE'S REALLY CARRYING THE NAME "AVENGERS" RIGHT NOW. NOT FORMALLY, AT LEAST AS FAR AS I'M CONCERNED.
GOLD STAR FOR THE FAN TURNED PRO.
(I CAN TELL.)
AND YOU'RE THE ONLY TEAM FOUNDER STILL ACTIVE, SO...
COUPLE OF YOU, I KNOW WELL. MOST OF YOU, NOT SO MUCH. BUT I DO FEEL LIKE WE RAISED EACH OTHERS' GAME TODAY.
AND I WOULD BE WILLING TO PLAY THAT OUT AND SEE WHERE IT GOES
YES.
IF ANYONE'S
YES.
INTERESTED.
YES.
WE HAVE NO FUNDS, WE HAVE NO EQUIPMENT, AND AT ANY MOMENT ULTRON OR KANG OR SOMEBODY COULD COME GUNNING FOR US. WITH THAT SAID--
--WHO WANTS TO JOIN ME AS AN AVENGER?

NOOOO!
SEE THE PRIMITIVE! I RECOGNIZE THAT UNIFORM FROM CHILDHOOD LESSONS.
ARE YOU A TEACHER, RE-ENACTING FOR US?
OR DID YOUR GODS OF MAGIC DISCARD YOU THROUGH THAT SPACE-TIME WARP?
TIME...?
HE...HE SAID NOTHING ABOUT TIME...! WHAT ERA IS THIS? WHERE DO YOU THINK I'M FROM?
DO WE LOOK TO YOU LIKE ANCIENT HISTORIANS?
ANCIENT--?
I WANTED TO LIVE FOREVER--TO HAVE MY NAME ECHO THROUGH HISTORY!
IT THINKS IT CAN WALK AMONG SOLDIERS, CHATTERING LIKE AN ANIMAL.
I WILL SHOW IT.
I AM WARBRIN--
CHUKK

EPILOGUE

VISION. WAIT.
I WANT TO THANK YOU.
FOR?
FOR...YOU KNOW...
FOR CONCEALING THE LIKELIHOOD THAT IT WAS YOUR PRESENCE WHICH DREW WARBRINGER HERE?
I'D...SAY "POSSIBILITY" MORE THAN "LIKELIHOOD," BUT--
REGARDLESS, IT CAN REMAIN OUR SECRET, SAMUEL...
I APPRECIATE--
...SO LONG AS YOU REMAIN AWARE THAT YOU ARE NOW IN MY DEBT.
HOLY CRAP.
I'M BEING BLACKMAILED.
BY AN AVENGER.

4

BRRINGGGGGG
SATURDAY.

INGGGGGKLIK
=SIGH=

=SIGH=

GET ALONG NOW, EDWIN. YOU DON'T WANT TO BE **LATE** YOUR **FIRST DAY.**
=SIGH=
YES, MOTHER.

JARVIS

=SIGH=
WELCOME TO NEW JERSEY
THE GARDEN STATE

STARK CONDEMNED AIRFIELD.

THERE HE IS! COME ON IN!
LADIES AND GENTLEMEN, MAY I PRESENT TO YOU THE ESTEEMED BUTLER OF LEGEND, MR. EDWIN JARVIS!

JARVIS--

--WELCOME TO
AVENGERS HEADQUARTERS!
=SIGH=

SUCH SECURITY.
YOU PASSED THROUGH A HEART-STOPPING ARRAY OF HIDDEN BIOMETRIC SENSORS AS YOU APPROACHED.
WE'RE UNFUNDED, NOT LAZY. HOW'S YOUR MOM?
STILL A BATTLESHIP, MR. STARK. SPEAKING OF WHICH, WHERE ARE YOU CONCEALING THE ACTUAL EQUIPMENT?
I THOUGHT I MIGHT BEGIN ACCLIMATING MYSELF TO--
=SIGH=
THIS IS THE KITCHEN...?
WELL...YEAH. BUT THROUGH HERE...
...THE NERVE CENTER. AS MUCH EQUIPMENT AS I COULD SALVAGE FROM THE OLD TOWER, BECAUSE CREDITORS.
NO MORE IDENTICARDS, BUT AT LEAST WE CAN STAY IN ENCRYPTED CONTACT VIA CELL PHONE.
I STILL HAVE A COUPLE OF SURVEILLANCE SATELLITES KICKING AROUND IN ORBIT, TOO. AND WE DO HAVE THE ONE QUINJET AND SOME ODDS AND ENDS.
YOU OKAY? YOU LOOK PALE.

...
IS VISION CREEPING YOU OUT LIKE HE CREE
YES!

DON'T BE SO CRYPTIC.
SORRY! I'VE JUST BEEN WANTING TO SAY THAT TO SOMEBODY, BUT... WHO AM I, YOU KNOW?
HE'S ONE OF THE BIG GUNS! I'M A FAN! BUT HE'S NOT AT ALL LIKE I EXPECTED! HE'S JUST--
ROBOTIC?

COLD. HE USED TO BE MARRIED! TO THE SCARLET WITCH! CAN YOU EVEN IMAGINE?
IT'S LIKE PICTURING AN IPAD IN WEDDED BLISS!
I LIKE HIM.
GHAAAH!
GHAAAH!

--BECAUSE YOU'RE PART OF THE TEAM, JARVIS. IT ISN'T THE AVENGERS WITHOUT YOU! YOU'RE NEEDED.
AROUND HERE? HARDLY, MR. STARK. THE CHILDREN CAN MICROWAVE THEIR OWN POPCORN, AND I'M SURE IF YOU TIED FEATHERS TO THEIR TAILS, THE FIELD MICE COULD DO THE DUSTING.
AND YOU CERTAINLY DON'T REQUIRE MY SERVICES...
...TO LOCATE A HURRICANE IN ATLANTIC CITY.
OH, MY GOD...
THERE WAS NO METEOROLOGICAL WARNING OF A STORM--WE WOULD HAVE BEEN ALERTED! WHERE DID THAT COME FR--
DOESN'T MATTER.

AVENGERS ASSEMBLE!
FINALLY, SOME ACTION...!
ALL TINGLY, ARE WE?
YOU'RE SUCH A JERK.
I'M REALLY NOT A--
LISTEN UP! HURRICANE OUT OF NOWHERE ON THE ATLANTIC CITY BOARDWALK, CASUALTIES MOUNTING!
QUINJET?
IT'S READY, BUT BY THE TIME WE ROLLED HER OUT, IT WOULDN'T SAVE US ANY TIME ON THIS SHORT A HOP!
WE HAVE FIVE FLIERS, TWO NON! MS. MARVEL, SPIDER-MAN, YOU GO WITH NOVA AND--
KRAKTOOM

CORRECTION: FOUR FLIERS AND ONE CANNONBALL.
LET'S GO! TRY TO KEEP UP WITH LADY LEAPS-INTO-DANGER, ALL RIGHT?
"THUNDER GOD OR NO, SHE'S GOING TO HAVE HER WORK CUT OUT FOR HER IF SHE CAN'T SHUT THAT WHIRLWIND DOWN!"

BY THE POWER OF THOR, GODDESS OF THUNDER, SUMMONER OF STORMS--
--I COMMAND THIS MAELSTROM TO CEASE IMMEDIATELY!
THWAM
LOOK OUT!
OW.
YOU ARE SOLID!
HA!
I AM BUILT FOR BATTLE!
IT CERTAINLY SEEMS TO BE YOUR PASSION!
CAN'T YOU GET THIS HURRICANE UNDER CONTROL?
SHE CAN'T, AND I CAN TELL YOU WHY! IT'S ARTIFICIAL!
SEE THAT MAN HOVERING IN THE EPICENTER?
I'VE GOT AN ENHANCED VISUAL, CROSS-REFERENCING OUR CASE FILES--

"--AND WE'RE DEALING WITH A TORNADO-BREWING MERC NAMED CYCLONE WHO'S BEEN TURNED UP TO ELEVEN!
"AND BELIEVE IT OR NOT--HE'S NOT OUR PRIORITY! THIS HAPPENED SO FAST--
"--PEOPLE DIDN'T HAVE TIME TO GET OUT OF THEIR CARS!"
OH, GOD.
HOW MANY?
APPROXIMATELY THIRTY-SEVEN VEHICLES!
OH, GOD!

NOVA, I MAY BE OF MORE USE UNENCUMBERED! TAKE HER!
WHAT? HIM? WAIT!
GOTCHA!

DO NOT BE ALARMED! HOLD ON TO ME TIGHTLY--

--AND I SHALL INCREASE MY DENSITY SO THAT WE MAY DROP UNAFFECTED BY THE WINDS.

THIS GUY SHOULD BE A PUSHOVER, BUT WE'LL NEVER WIN IF WE KEEP PLAYING DEFENSE!
I'LL GRAB MORE BYSTANDERS, YOU TWO TAKE OUT THE WINDBAG!
YOU'RE NOT OUR BOSS!

SHE REMINDS ME MORE OF HERCULES THAN SHE DOES OF THOR ODINSON.
REMEMBER WHEN WE SAW HER EAT AN ENTIRE SIDE OF BEEF?
I WISH I LOVED ANYTHING AS MUCH AS SHE LOVES... EVERYTHING.
HA!
USE YOUR ELECTRO-STING-WONK!
I CAN'T WITH YOU TOUCHING HIM!
DON'T TROUBLE YOURSELVES.
I WAS JUST LEAVING.
THWIPP
YOU'RE KILLING PEOPLE! WHY? THEY DIDN'T DO ANYTHING TO YOU!
I'M A HIRED GUN!

"MY ORDER WAS TO LEVEL THE CASINOS!
"BODY COUNT ISN'T MY PROBLEM--
"NOT FOR WHAT THE DYNASTY IS PAYING ME!"
FLING ME AT HIM!
NO! YOU MISS, HE'LL SWAT YOU DEAD!
I KNOW THE RISKS!
JUST DO IT!

WHAM
WHAM
WHAM
WHAM
NICE! YOU EVER CONSIDER A CAREER IN THE MMA?
YOU GOT HIM!
NOT HARDLY, KIDS.
LET'S SEE HOW DEEP I CAN SINK YOU INTO THE PAVEMENT.
THOOM

TELL US MORE ABOUT THIS "DYNASTY" OR FACE THE CONSEQUENCES.
OH, SPLENDID. ANOTHER EMPTY THREAT.
IMAGINE THE DAMAGE YOU'LL DO ONCE I THROW YOU THROUGH THE TROPICANA.
WHAT... WHAT ARE YOU...?
DENSE.

IS HE--?
HE'LL JUST BE UNCONSCIOUS UNTIL WE START TO SHAKE SOME INFORMATION OUT OF HIM. EVERYONE ELSE OKAY?

=KAFF=
...NO BROKEN BONES... I PROTECTED MS. MARVEL FROM THE IMPACT...
...DON'T... FLATTER YOURSELF...

NONSENSE! YOU WERE BOTH SHIELDED BY THE LUSTY BLOOD-RUSH OF HEROIC COMBAT!
THOR IS VERY...HIGH-SPIRITED TODAY.

WHOOP-DE-DOO. RESCUED BY THE UNDERSTUDY AVENGERS!
WHERE ARE THE REAL ONES? MAN, THE WORLD'S GETTIN' SO POLITICALLY CORRECT THESE DAYS...!
DID YOU HEAR THAT? AFTER WE SAVED THEIR LIVES?
LET THEM BE UNGRATEFUL. WHAT DOES IT MATTER?

I KNOW, I KNOW. IT'S JUST... I'M TRYING TO REACH PEOPLE, YOU KNOW? AND SOMETIMES IT FEELS IMPOSSIBLE.
YOU HAVEN'T TOLD US WHERE YOU COME FROM, BUT YOU MUST GET THE "WHEN'S THE REAL ONE COMING BACK?" CRACKS, TOO. DOESN'T THAT GET UNDER YOUR SKIN SOMETIMES?
HA. FROM ONE WARRIOR TO ANOTHER, CAPTAIN...

...YOU FRET TOO MUCH.
YOU CERTAINLY TASTE LIKE I WOULD IMAGINE A CAPTAIN AMERICA TO TASTE.
...
YOU... TASTE LIKE...
...LIKE A GODDESS...

DID YOU NOT ENJOY IT?
...ABSOLUTELY...
...BUT... WHY...
BECAUSE I FELT LIKE IT.
ALWAYS ACT ON YOUR IMPULSES, SAM WILSON. LIFE'S CANDLE BURNS TOO BRIEFLY NOT TO LIVE IN THE MOMENT.
AVENGERS! UNTIL OUR PATHS CROSS AGAIN...
AN ODD SENTIMENT COMING FROM AN IMMORTAL...
CAP?
...
CAP, WE SHOULD HELP CLEAN UP.
...
GIVE ME A SECOND.
WOW.
JEALOUS?
NO!
LIAR.

CLEANUP SOUNDS DOABLE, THOUGH NOT MY FAVORITE WAY TO SPEND A SATURDAY AFTERNOON.
I'LL MAKE SURE CYCLONE STICKS AROUND WHILE WE...
...WHILE WE...
SKREEUNK
YOU TRAILED OFF.
SORRY. IT JUST HIT ME.
"LIFE'S CANDLE BURNS TOO BRIEFLY." I REALIZE WE DON'T KNOW MUCH ABOUT OUR NEW ALLY...
"...BUT NOW THAT VISION'S MENTIONED IT...
"...THAT IS AN AWFULLY STRANGE THING FOR A SUPPOSED IMMORTAL TO SAY, AND IT MAKES ME NERVOUS.
"IS SHE REALLY WHO SHE CLAIMS TO BE...?"

GET OUT, MS. MARVEL. YOU ARE NO LONGER AN AVENGER!
5

AVENGERS HANGAR.
24 HOURS AGO.
POWER UPGRADE COMPLETE. RECORDING RESULTS. COMMENCE TESTING OF HOLOGRAPHIC IMAGE CAPABILITIES.
UPGRADE SUCCESSFUL.
SZKKKKKK
RECORDED RESULTS ELIMINATED.

WE COULD HAVE SUMMONED BACKUP. THE AVENGERS WILL ALWAYS HEED THE CALL OF CAPTAIN AMERICA.
I KNOW, BUT I...
...I GUESS I'M GLAD IT'S JUST THE TWO OF US.
YOU KISSED ME YESTERDAY, THOR. WE...SHARED A MOMENT. DO PEOPLE SAY THINGS LIKE THAT IN ASGARD? IS THAT WHAT YOU'D CALL IT? A MOMENT?
NOT IF IT LASTS.
WHERE... WHERE ARE YOU TAKING ME...?
TO MY PLACE.

ASGARD.
IT'S BEAUTIFUL. YOU'RE BEAUTIFUL.
IT'S FUNNY. WE DON'T EVEN REALLY KNOW EACH OTHER UNDER THE MASKS.
I'M SAM. SAM WILSON.
AND I...
...I AM CAPTAIN MARVEL.
WOW.
YOU REALLY ARE A GODDESS.
I AM A WOMAN.
SAME THING.
THOR?
THOR, MY LOVE...HOW COULD YOU...?
STOP.

longing for the taste of one another's lips seemingly rewarded.
Suddenly, from beyond the waterfall's glow stepped the Juggernaut, his face a mask
lousy and betrayal.
"SUDDENLY, FROM BEYOND THE WATERFALL'S GLOW STEPPED THE JUGGERNAUT, HIS FACE A MASK OF JEALOUSY AND BETRAYAL."
YOU AND YOUR SHIP-FIC. HE ALREADY HAS A MASK. ALSO, HOW DID THE JUGGERNAUT GET TO ASGARD? ISN'T IT IN, LIKE, ANOTHER DIMENSION?
FOUR HOURS AGO.
NOTHING CAN STOP THE JUGGERNAUT.
CERTAINLY NOT UNREQUITED ROMANCE, CLEARLY. AT WHAT POINT DO THEY ALL RIDE AWAY ON WINGED PONIES?
KAMALA! NO BOYS IN YOUR ROOM! YOU KNOW FATHER'S RULES!
'SUP, AAMIR.
'SUP, BRUNO.
THE DOOR IS OPEN, AAMIR! GO AWAY!
BESIDES, WHY WOULD YOU WRITE AVENGERS FANFIC WHEN YOU CAN NOW LIVE IT?
BASED ON TRUE EVENTS! THEY KISSED. I SAW IT.
WHAT?
TELL YOU LATER. GO. I'M GOING TO BE LATE FOR AN AVENGERS MEETING.
DO YOU NEED BUS FARE?
"DON'T WORRY ABOUT IT.

THWIPP
"I'VE GOT A RIDE."
WOOHOOOO!
PLEASE KEEP YOUR SEATS AND TRAY TABLES IN THEIR UPRIGHT POSITION.
I LOVE MY LIFE!

HMM.
TWO HOURS AGO.
AVENGERS ASSEMBLE?
PRETTY PLEASE?
SHRAKK
THE OTHERS ARE OCCUPIED WITH APPREHENDING THE MAD THINKER AND PROTECTING CIVILIANS, MS. MARVEL.
IT IS OUR RESPONSIBILITY TO DEAL WITH THINKER'S DREADBOT!

'KAY.
REMEMBER... WHAT CAP...TAUGHT YOU ABOUT...JUDO-- NNNGGH--!
KATHOOOM
WHO'S NEXT? WHAT? NO TAKERS? WELL, THEN...!

NOW.
...NO...
...NO, NO, NO...
...THERE'S SOME MISTAKE...
THE MISTAKE WAS OURS. AND NOW WE RECTIFY IT.
UNFORTUNATELY FOR YOU, YOUNG LADY, THE VISION SAYS HE CAN NOW PLAY BACK ANYTHING LOGGED IN HIS MEMORIES.
VISION, IF YOU WOULD...?
REMEMBER... WHAT CAP... TAUGHT YOU...
AAAAH!
AAAAH!

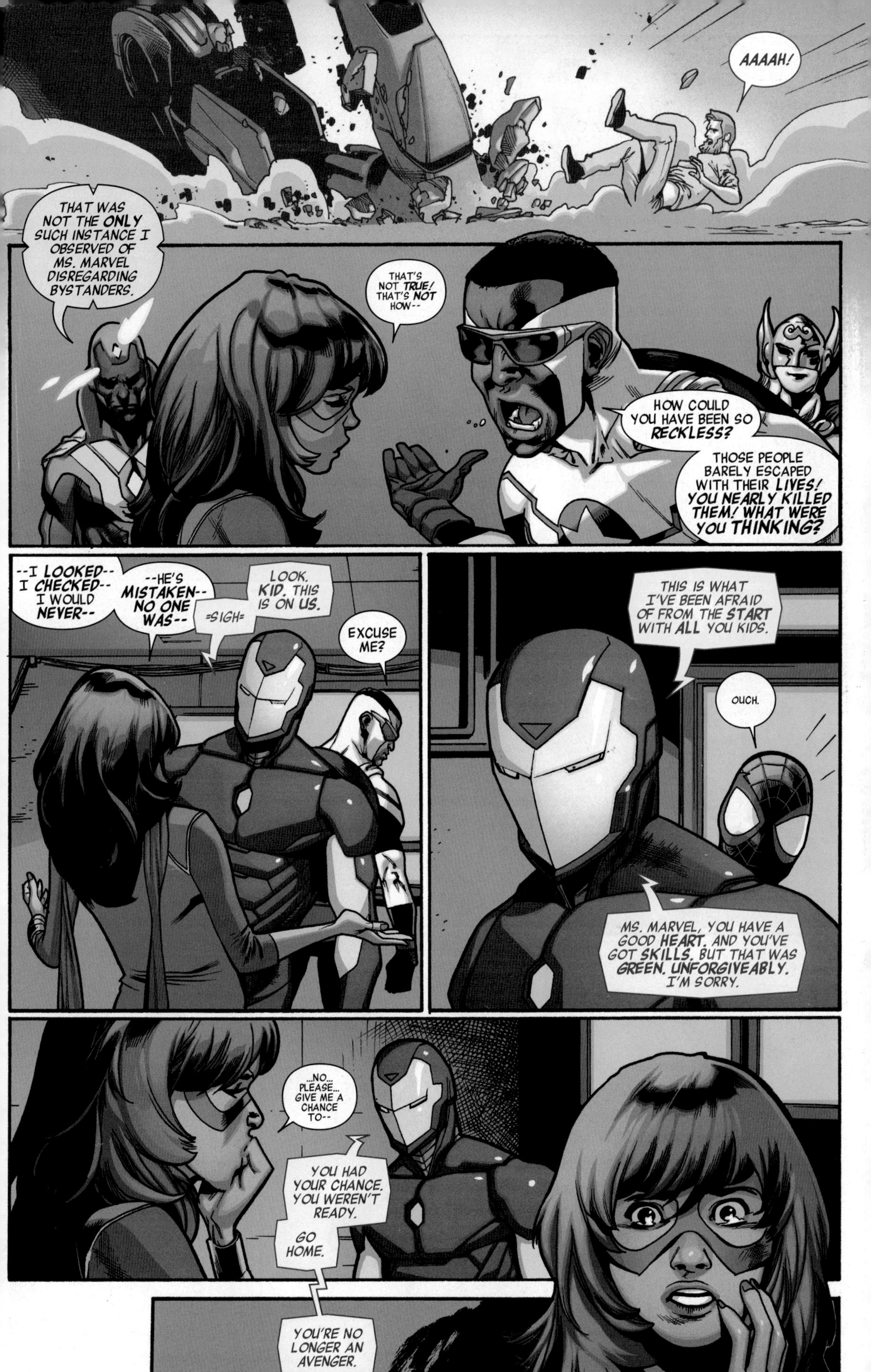
AAAAH!
THAT WAS NOT THE ONLY SUCH INSTANCE I OBSERVED OF MS. MARVEL DISREGARDING BYSTANDERS.
THAT'S NOT TRUE! THAT'S NOT HOW--
HOW COULD YOU HAVE BEEN SO RECKLESS?
THOSE PEOPLE BARELY ESCAPED WITH THEIR LIVES! YOU NEARLY KILLED THEM! WHAT WERE YOU THINKING?
--I LOOKED-- I CHECKED-- I WOULD NEVER--
--HE'S MISTAKEN-- NO ONE WAS--
=SIGH=
LOOK. KID. THIS IS ON US.
EXCUSE ME?
THIS IS WHAT I'VE BEEN AFRAID OF FROM THE START WITH ALL YOU KIDS.
OUCH.
MS. MARVEL, YOU HAVE A GOOD HEART. AND YOU'VE GOT SKILLS. BUT THAT WAS GREEN. UNFORGIVEABLY. I'M SORRY.
...NO... PLEASE... GIVE ME A CHANCE TO--
YOU HAD YOUR CHANCE. YOU WEREN'T READY.
GO HOME.
YOU'RE NO LONGER AN AVENGER.

SORRY I'M LATE! I--
HEY!
WHAT'D I MISS? WHAT'S WRONG WITH YOU?
SOMETHING'S WRONG WITH THE VISION AND HE'S LYING ABOUT ME AND THEY WOULDN'T LISTEN AND THEY THREW ME OUT AND-- AND--

--AND YOU CAN BE HAPPY NOW!
ME? WHAT DID I--?

YOU'VE ALWAYS BEEN A JERK TO ME! YOU NEVER WANTED ME AROUND, AND NOW YOU WIN!
...VISION...

I NEVER PROMISED I WOULD KEEP YOUR SECRET, NOVA. WHETHER I DIVULGE IT OR NOT DEPENDS ENTIRELY UPON YOU.

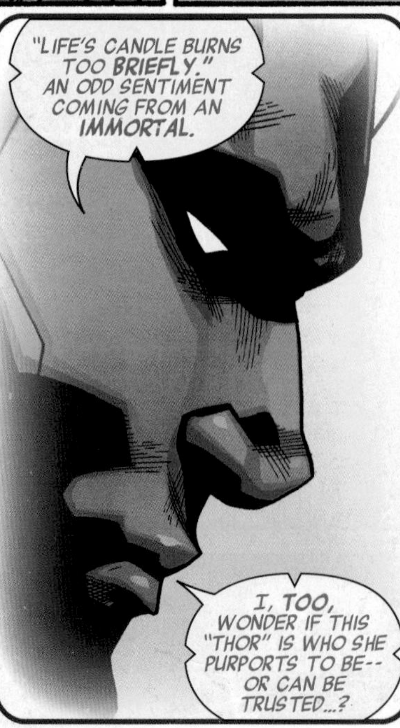
"LIFE'S CANDLE BURNS TOO BRIEFLY." AN ODD SENTIMENT COMING FROM AN IMMORTAL.
I, TOO, WONDER IF THIS "THOR" IS WHO SHE PURPORTS TO BE-- OR CAN BE TRUSTED...?

=KOFF=
THAT SEEMED... HARSH.
OH, REALLY?
I'LL JUST STAY QUIET NOW...
VISION! WHAT DID YOU DO TO HER?
NOVA--?
HE'S SCREWING WITH US! MESSING WITH OUR HEADS! HE'S POISON! HE'S--
CALM YOURSELF, YOUNGLING! AVENGERS DO NOT COME TO BLOWS WITH ONE ANOTHER! SHOW RESPECT!
TO HIM?! CAN'T YOU SEE? I DON'T KNOW WHY, BUT HE'S PLAYING US--LIKE IT'S A BIG GAME TO HIM!
SAM, YOU ARE OUT OF LINE! NOT ONLY WOULDN'T THE VISION DO THAT... HE CAN'T DO THAT!
HE'S A CREATURE OF LOGIC, KID.
HE'S NO MORE CAPABLE OF DECEPTION THAN A SUBARU. NO OFFENSE, VIZ.
OH, YEAH? HE'S SURE HAD A HOLD OVER ME, THAT--

PRIORITY ALERT
PRIORITY ALERT
GREAT DAY FOR JARVIS TO TAKE OFF. WHO'S ON MONITORS?
PRIORITY ALERT
PRIORITY ALERT
LET MY A.I. FILL US IN.
SOME SORT OF DISTURBANCE IN HIGH LINE PARK. SOMETHING HUGE.
LET'S GO, PEOPLE. SPIDEY, YOU RIDE WITH VISION.
I'LL TAKE POINT--
NO. WE'RE SURE AS HELL NOT TAKING A WILD CARD INTO BATTLE.
I--I WANT TO HELP--
I DON'T NEED THE HEADACHE! I DON'T NEED YOUR TANTRUMS! YOU COME BURSTING IN HERE ATTACKING AND ACCUSING AND--
YOU KNOW WHAT? MY PATIENCE IS SHOT! YOU'RE NO LONGER WELCOME HERE, EITHER! GET OUT!
...
WHAT?

KIDS, AM I RIGHT?
DON'T YOU START WITH ME. BEING AN AVENGER IS A RESPONSIBILITY. THOSE TWO COULDN'T HANDLE IT.
THEY'LL LEARN, BUT NOT ON THE JOB. NOT WHEN LIVES ARE AT STAKE.
LET'S CHANGE THE SUBJECT, THEN. YOU AND GOLDILOCKS. YOU ENJOYED IT?
THE KISS? FROM THOR? I HAVE ZERO COMPLAINTS. BUT IT DIDN'T MEAN ANYTHING. THE HEAT OF ADRENALINE. THAT'S ALL.
JUST BE COOL. DON'T GET WEIRD ABOUT IT.
I DON'T NEED YOUR ADVICE ABOUT WOMEN, TONY.
REMEMBER THAT, LIKE ODINSON, THERE'S PROBABLY MORE TO HER THAN SHE LETS ON. GODS HAVE A WAY OF SURPRISING US MERE MORTALS.
SO NOTED. CAN WE TALK ABOUT SOMETHING ELSE?

FRIDAY, CAN YOU GIVE ME AN I.D.?
LIKE WHO THE HELL THAT IS?

EQUINOX. FOCUSED CONTROL OF TEMPERATURE EXTREMES.
EQUINOX, EVERYBODY! THOUGHT HE LOOKED FAMILIAR, BUT I DON'T REMEMBER HIM PUNCHING UP THIS EFFECTIVELY!
SOMEBODY WANT TO SMACK HIM LIKE A WRECKING BALL, THEN?
UNNECESSARY.
THE REST OF YOU CONCENTRATE ON CONTAINING THE DAMAGE HE HAS CAUSED. DESPITE HIS COMMAND OVER FIRE AND FROST--

--EQUINOX IS HARDLY AN AVENGERS-LEVEL THREAT THIS DAY--
SKRAAK-KK-K
OH, NO...?
WHAT ABOUT THE EQUINOX FROM TOMORROW?

OR THE DAY AFTER THAT?
PORTALS, PORTALS EVERYWHERE! WHO SAID "SEND IN THE CLONES"? AND ARE THOSE PIECES OF OUR GEAR HE'S--THEY'RE--CARRYING...?
THEY ARE STILL OUTNUMBERED.
IT DOESN'T MATTER. THE AVENGERS ARE DESTINED TO LOSE THIS BATTLE. WE KNOW...

...BECAUSE WE'RE FROM THE *FUTURE!*

EVERYONE **FALL BACK!**
HONOR THE *DYNASTY.*
HONOR THE *DYNASTY.*
HONOR THE *DYNASTY.*
HONOR THE *DYNASTY.*
HONOR THE DYNASTY.
HONOR THE DYNASTY.
"**DYNASTY.**" OUR FOES HAVE MADE **MENTION** OF THIS **BEFORE**, HAVEN'T THEY? THE **QENG DYNASTY?**
HONOR THE *DYNASTY.*

"...FROM THE FUTURE..."
NO. NOT "QENG."

KANG.
THE CONQUEROR OF TIME.
STAND FAST, AVENGERS! THE ODDS REMAIN IN OUR FAVOR SO LONG AS WE REMAIN TOGETHER!
=HNNNH!=
UHH...
...VISION...?

NO!
HWWFFF!
THOOM THOOM
MY HAMMER! I MUST REGAIN MY HAMMER!
THAT WOULD BE GREAT, BUT RIGHT NOW, WE NEED YOUR MUSCLE! WE'RE IN THE FUTURE, AND THEY'RE STILL COMING!

THOOM THOOM
SO FOCUS AND FIGHT!
YOU DO NOT UNDERSTAND! IF MJOLNIR AND I ARE SEPARATED FOR TOO LONG A TIME, I--

FAAASH

--I CHANGE BACK--
--INTO *THIS*--!

6

MANHATTAN, NOW.
WHAT DO YOU WANT, KANG?
HONOR THE DYNASTY.
HONOR THE DYNASTY.
HONOR THE DYNASTY.
HONOR THE DYNASTY.
SEE, THERE'S YOUR FIRST MISTAKE.
I'M NOT KANG.
WELL, KIND OF. BUT NOT EXACTLY.
"THERE'S BEEN A...GLITCH IN THE TIMESTREAM.
"SOMETHING HAPPENED TO DIVIDE ME. US. SPIN ME OFF.
"TO BE HONEST, I'M NOT SURE WHICH OF US IS THE REAL CONQUEROR OF TIME NOW.
"WHAT I DO KNOW IS THAT I'M TRAPPED HERE IN YOUR BACKWATER CENTURY BEHIND SOME BIZARRE FIREWALL OF TIME..."
...AND I'M NOT WILLING TO SLEEP FOR TWO THOUSAND YEARS JUST TO GET HOME AGAIN.
I CAN TIMESHIFT OTHER THINGS, OTHER PEOPLE--JUST NOT MYSELF.

"THEREFORE I PLAN TO CREATE MY OWN DYNASTY IN YOUR ERA.
"THAT'S WHY I ENLISTED CYCLONE AND THE RADIOACTIVE MAN. BUT THAT'S A MAKE-DO. THE PAYOFF WON'T BE FOR TWENTY CENTURIES YET.
"WHICH IS WHY I WAS SO HOT TO GRAB THAT CHITAURAN ARTIFACT-- UNTIL YOU SHATTERED IT.
"WARBRINGER DIDN'T REALIZE IT BREACHED TIME AS WELL AS SPACE.
"SEEING THE AVENGERS IN ACTION, HOWEVER, REMINDED ME I HAD ANOTHER OPTION."
DOES KANG ALWAYS TALK THIS MUCH? WHY IS HE DOING THE WHOLE "EXPLAIN MY VILLAINY" SPEECH?
BECAUSE MY VICTORY IS PREORDAINED, AND YOU'RE NOT A THREAT.
TO GET WHAT I'M HERE FOR, I HAVE A SECRET WEAPON TO PROTECT ME--
NYAAAAH!
--AND HIS NAME IS THE VISION.

SUBURBAN NEW JERSEY, NOW.
IF THEY'RE GOING TO KICK YOU OUT, THEY COULD AT LEAST DRIVE YOU HOME.
?
I THINK YOU HAVE ME CONFUSED WITH SOMEONE ELSE.
RELAX, MS. MARVEL. I'M NOT LOOKING AT YOUR FACE. BESIDES, RIGHT NOW WE HAVE MORE IN COMMON THAN OUR SECRET IDENTITY PARANOIA.

LEAVE ME ALONE.
THEY BOOTED ME, TOO.
YOU? WHY?
BECAUSE I WENT ALL HAM ON THE VISION. I THINK HE DID FRAME YOU FOR THAT WHOLE "ENDANGERING BYSTANDERS" CHARGE. I KNOW HE DID.
WHY DO YOU BELIEVE ME?
BECAUSE HE'S BEEN BLACKMAILING ME FROM DAY ONE.
WHAT? WHAT DID YOU DO?

I LIKE THE AUTOMATIC PRESUMPTION THAT I'M THE ONE AT FAULT RATHER THAN THE ANDROID WHO JUST CRATERED YOU.
SORRY.
WARBRINGER? I'D FOUGHT HIM BEFORE. I WANTED TO TELL THE AVENGERS THAT HE MAYBE CAME TO EARTH BECAUSE HE WANTED REVENGE ON ME, BUT--
I DON'T THINK THAT WAS WHY HE CAME HERE.
WELL, I SHOULD HAVE SPOKEN UP ANYWAY. I WAS JUST SCARED THEY'D BE PISSED. I WAS GONNA, BUT VISION TIPPED TO IT AND STEERED ME OUT OF IT.
THEN, WHEN I WENT TO THANK HIM FOR COVERING, HE STARTED MAKING THESE VEILED THREATS THAT I OWED HIM.
YOU DIDN'T SAY ANYTHING ABOUT THAT?
WHO WOULD BELIEVE ME?
I DO, NOW.
TURN AROUND.
IF SOMETHING'S WRONG WITH THE VISION, MAYBE HE'S AFTER ALL THE AVENGERS.
WE HAVE TO HELP THEM.
PRESUMING THEY DON'T SEND US TO THE NEGATIVE ZONE AS STALKERS.
FOR THE AVENGERS? I'LL TAKE THAT RISK.

VISION, WE TRUSTED YOU!
THAT WAS CERTAINLY THE PLAN. AFTER THE WARBRINGER FAILURE, I REALIZED IT WOULD HELP TO HAVE AT LEAST ONE AVENGER ON THE INSIDE. I LOOKED BACK IN THE RECENT PAST FOR A VULNERABLE MOMENT--
"--AND PLANTED SOME PROTOCOLS INSIDE VISION'S COMPUTER BRAIN.*
"MY LITTLE PUPPET AND I HAVE BEEN PLAYING A LONG GAME TO FRAGMENT AND DESTROY THE AVENGERS--"
*DURING THE EVENTS OF AVENGERS #0. --TOM

--LEAVING WHAT I'M AFTER UNGUARDED.
NOW, WHERE...?
AH.

THERE YOU ARE.

I DON'T GET IT. WHAT DOES HE WANT WITH THOR'S HAMMER?
OF COURSE.

MANHATTAN, THE NEAR FUTURE.
IT CAN TRAVEL THROUGH TIME.
MJOLNIR?
HONOR THE DYNASTY!
HONOR THE DYNASTY!
HONOR THE DYNASTY!
SHZAAK
I'M PICKING YOU UP, OKAY? LET ME KNOW IF I HURT YOU.
WE HAVE TO GET YOU OUT OF HERE...
JANE.
...JANE.
WAIT. JANE FOSTER? DOCTOR JANE FOSTER. WE MET...
...BEFORE THE CANCER.
JEEZ.
OKAY, NEITHER OF US IS GOING TO LIVE THROUGH THIS DOGPILE WITH YOU IN THIS STATE. WE HAVE TO FIGURE OUT HOW TO REUNITE YOU WITH YOUR HAMMER--
--AND I CAN HELP WITH THAT.

YOU CANNOT LIFT MJOLNIR, KANG.
I DON'T HAVE TO MOVE IT TO SIPHON IT. STAND GUARD.

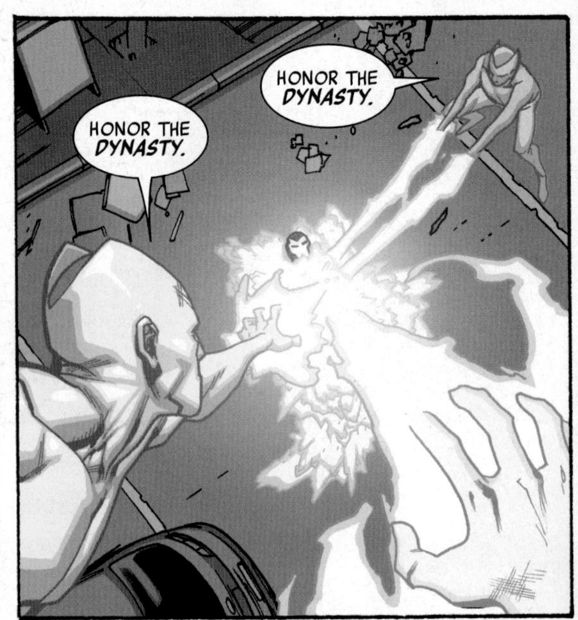
HONOR THE DYNASTY.
HONOR THE DYNASTY.

AAAAAH!

HONOR THGGGG--
OH, YOU MEAN THE DYNASTY THAT WAS ENDED BY CAPTAIN AMERICA'S BIRD?
GO, REDWING!

VERY WELL. I HAD PLANNED TO KILL IRON MAN FIRST... BUT I THINK I JUST CHANGED MY MIND.

LEAVE REDWING ALONE!

HE'S THE ONLY AVENGER WHO STILL LIKES ME.
GUESS WE'RE ENEMIES NOW.
I DON'T LIKE THE WAY THIS DAY IS TURNING OUT AT ALL.
THWAM
WHATEVER HAPPENS NOW, VISION--
"--WE HAD DAMN WELL BETTER GET CAP AND THOR BACK!"
WHERE... ARE YOU TAKING ME...?
HEAR ME OUT! ONLY YOU CAN LIFT MJOLNIR, YES? WHICH MEANS THAT IT DOESN'T MATTER HOW FAR IN THE FUTURE WE WERE BLASTED--
--IF WE'RE LUCKY--
--IT HAS TO STILL BE WHERE IT FELL WHEN YOU LEFT IT BEHIND!
TO...
...TO ME...

SKRAKOOM

GNNGH!
THAM
JANE...?
JANE, WAKE UP...!
JANE...!

WHO ARE THESE GUYS?
HONOR THE DYNASTY.
I DON'T WANT MY LAST WORDS TO BE A TIME-TRAVEL LECTURE!
BUT ACCORDING TO MY SPIDER-SENSE, THERE'S NOT A ONE OF THEM WHO DOESN'T WANT US...
...DEAD...
...
HONOR THE DYNASTY.

ALL HAIL KANG!
HONOR THE DYNASTY!
WHAT THE--?

...YOU.
YOU'RE THE PRESENT-DAY EQUINOX!
I TAKE YOU OUT OF THE FIGHT--
THWAM

TFFF
TFFF
TFFF
TFFF
TFFF
TFFF
?
--AND THERE IS NO YOU TO COME FROM THE FUTURE!
HOW DID YOU KNOW WHICH ONE TO HIT?
ALL THE OTHERS WERE FUTURE VERSIONS OF HIM! THAT MEANS THEY ALL HAD A MEMORY OF ME GOING ALL KANG-IFIED!
THE ONE I PUNCHED WAS THE ONLY ONE WHO SUDDENLY STOPPED TINGLING MY SPIDER-SENSE, EXCUSE THE EXPRESSION--
"--BECAUSE HE WAS THE ONLY ONE WHO WAS SURPRISED!"
TFFF
JANE, QUICK--
TFFF
TFFF
--GIVE ME YOUR HAND!

WHAT'S THE MATTER, VISION?
WANT TO POP MY HEART, BUT CAN'T BREAK THROUGH MY ARMOR?
BRUTE FORCE WILL NOT BE NECESSARY WITH AN IMMATERIAL--
EYAAAARGH!
--HAND. CONNECTED TO YOUR NERVOUS SYSTEM--CONNECTED TO YOUR BRAIN--
--CONNECTED TO THE SYSTEM REBOOT I JUST DOWNLOADED FROM THE AVENGERS' DATACLOUD.
SORRY, PAL.
MR. GRYPHON IS KANG? KANG THE CONQUEROR?
AGAIN, I WILL RECAP LATER!
HE'S BUILT SOME SORT OF TIME-ENERGY SHIELD!
WE CAN'T GET THROUGH!

THAT'S X-MEN TALK.
WE'RE THE AVENGERS.
LET'S PROVE IT.

AVENGERS ASSEMBLE.
LATE TO THE PARTY, FOLKS.
CLEVER TO TAKE THE HAMMER FROM THE FUTURE, THOUGH. THE TIME PARADOX IS GIVING ME A MIGRAINE.
LET'S SEE IF I CAN SPREAD THE PAIN AROUND.

TAKE IT FROM AN EXPERIENCED CHRONAL TRAVELER.
NOTHING IN THE UNIVERSE IS QUITE AS AGONIZING AS BEING DRAGGED UP AND DOWN YOUR OWN TIMELINE.
I HAVE TO GO NOW. THE OTHER EVENTS I'VE PUT INTO MOTION HERE REAP WORLD-SHATTERING BENEFITS TWO MILLENNIA FROM NOW.
YES, I'LL BE BACK--WITH REINFORCEMENTS THAT WOULD LEAVE YOU SLACK-JAWED--
--BUT YOU WON'T LIVE TO SEE THEM.
HKKK!
RELEASE.
THEM.

YOU DEFY ME? I ORDER YOU TO STAND ASIDE!
YOU FORCED ME TO BETRAY MY FRIENDS!
YOU TURNED ME INTO AN INSTRUMENT OF DESTRUCTION!
YOU WILL PAY FOR THOSE CRIMES!
DIDN'T SOMEONE SAY VISION HAD PURGED HIS EMOTIONS?
APPARENTLY HE'S BUILDING NEW ONES!
THEN THEY'LL TEAR EACH OTHER APART--AND WHO KNOWS WHAT ELSE THEY'LL TAKE WITH THEM!
HE SAID HE WAS VULNERABLE TO TIME PARADOXES! HOW DO YOU WEAPONIZE THOSE?
LIKE THIS.

KLANGA-LANGG
HYAAAAH!
THIS IS NOT OVER, AVENGERS!
I SWEAR TO YOU--
--THIS IS NOT O--

CHOOM
THAT WAS...WAY TOO CLOSE...
HELP HIM UP!
HE WEIGHS A TON.
THAT'S HIS POWER. READ THE HANDBOOK SOMETIME.
VISION? BUDDY? YOU ALL CLEAR?
I...
...I'M NOT CERTAIN HOW BEST TO PROCESS THIS. I DID NOTHING WRONG OF MY OWN VOLITION, YET I FEEL...REGRET. SHAME.
I APOLOGIZE FOR MY ACTIONS.
I HOPE YOU CAN FORGIVE ME.
...
I...
YEAH.

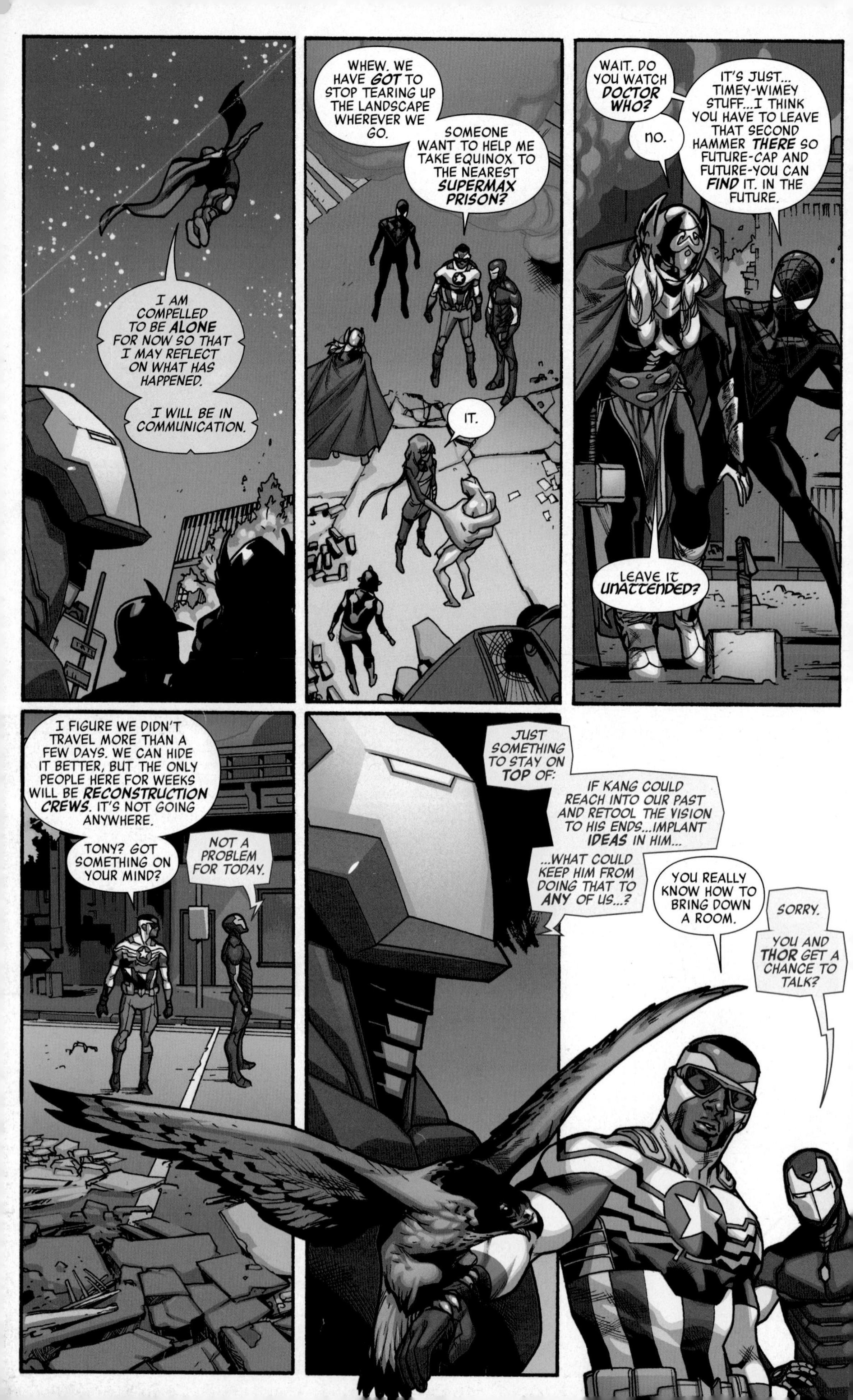
I AM COMPELLED TO BE ALONE FOR NOW SO THAT I MAY REFLECT ON WHAT HAS HAPPENED.
I WILL BE IN COMMUNICATION.
WHEW. WE HAVE GOT TO STOP TEARING UP THE LANDSCAPE WHEREVER WE GO.
SOMEONE WANT TO HELP ME TAKE EQUINOX TO THE NEAREST SUPERMAX PRISON?
IT.
WAIT. DO YOU WATCH DOCTOR WHO?
no.
IT'S JUST... TIMEY-WIMEY STUFF...I THINK YOU HAVE TO LEAVE THAT SECOND HAMMER THERE SO FUTURE-CAP AND FUTURE-YOU CAN FIND IT. IN THE FUTURE.
LEAVE IT UNATTENDED?
I FIGURE WE DIDN'T TRAVEL MORE THAN A FEW DAYS. WE CAN HIDE IT BETTER, BUT THE ONLY PEOPLE HERE FOR WEEKS WILL BE RECONSTRUCTION CREWS. IT'S NOT GOING ANYWHERE.
TONY? GOT SOMETHING ON YOUR MIND?
NOT A PROBLEM FOR TODAY.
JUST SOMETHING TO STAY ON TOP OF:
IF KANG COULD REACH INTO OUR PAST AND RETOOL THE VISION TO HIS ENDS...IMPLANT IDEAS IN HIM...
...WHAT COULD KEEP HIM FROM DOING THAT TO ANY OF US...?
YOU REALLY KNOW HOW TO BRING DOWN A ROOM.
SORRY.
YOU AND THOR GET A CHANCE TO TALK?

"NOT YET."
...TREATMENT...
HI.
OH.
NO, THANK YOU. I CAN'T WHILE I'M TAKING...
SAM? I DIDN'T EXPECT...
WHO ELSE IS WITH YOU?
NOBODY. YOUR SECRET'S SAFE.
I WANTED YOU TO KNOW THAT.
THAT'S IMPORTANT TO ME.
OBVIOUSLY.
NOW... CAN WE TALK ABOUT WHY...?
NEXT: AVENGERS VS. AVENGERS!

FREE COMIC BOOK DAY 2015 (AVENGERS) #1

A SPECIAL PEEK INTO THE FUTURE OF THE NEW MARVEL UNIVERSE!
AVENGERS ASSEMBLE!
ARE WE ALLOWED TO SAY THAT YET?
I'VE BEEN WAITING ALL MY LIFE!
SAYS THE HIGH-SCHOOL STUDENT. I HAVE SHIRTS OLDER THAN YOU.
NOVA. SPIDEY. ME, MS. MARVEL.
OUR FIRST DAY AS AVENGERS--

TEN MINUTES LATER.
I GAVE YOU ONE ORDER.
--AND OUR LAST.

TEN MINUTES AGO.
MANHATTAN'S FEDERAL RESERVE BANK.
OUT OF NOWHERE, IT CAME...
THOR! VISION! FIND OUT JUST HOW TOUGH THAT THING IS!
CAP AND I WILL RUN DEFENSE!
MS. MARVEL, NOVA, SPIDEY--

--LESSON ONE: WHY WOULD ANYONE DROP A FIRE-BREATHING DRAGON OUTSIDE A BUILDING LIKE THIS?
BECAUSE IT'S HEAVY?
TO SHOW OFF?
TO KEEP ANYONE ELSE FROM GOING IN?
WEB-HEAD FOR THE WIN! EXACTLY! SOMEONE'S INSIDE WHO DOESN'T WANT TO BE FOLLOWED! FIND OUT WHO, TAKE HIM OR HER OUT IF YOU CAN, BUT ABOVE ALL--
--ABOVE ALL--DO NOT, UNDER ANY CIRCUMSTANCES, LET THEM GET AWAY!
I WAS GOING TO SAY "DISTRACTION"!
WHAT'S YOUR POWER AGAIN? 20/20 HINDSIGHT?
MINE'S CAMOUFLAGE.
MINE IS STAYING FOCUSED. TRY IT.
SNFF SNFF
DO YOU GUYS SMELL THAT? IT'S AWFUL-- LIKE...
...
...OH, NO...

UNBELIEVABLE!
THE BEAST'S HIDE IS TOUGHER THAN ASGARDIAN STEEL!
THEN PERHAPS THE MORE EFFECTIVE ATTACK--
--IS FROM WITHIN.
IRON MAN, MY ENERGY CELLS DO NOT RECHARGE AS SWIFTLY AS THEY ONCE DID! IF YOU COULD PROVIDE A BOOST--?
ANYTHING THAT'LL SLOW THIS MONSTER DOWN! ANY OTHER IDEAS? ANYONE?
HELL, I BET CAPTAIN AMERICA WOULD EVEN TAKE STEVE ROGERS' ADVICE AT THIS POINT!
DON'T EVEN JOKE.
YEP, GUESS THAT'S STILL A THING. JUST CHECKING. VISION!
"WHAT DO YOU SEE IN THERE? WHAT'S GOING ON?"

BODIES... EVERYWHERE...
WE'RE...WE'RE AVENGERS...
...WE SHOULD HAVE BEEN ABLE TO STOP THIS BEFORE...
STOP WHAT?
THE COLLAPSE OF THE WESTERN ECONOMY?
THE RISE OF THE NEW QENG DYNASTY?
YOU ARE NOW WITNESS TO THE BEGINNING OF SOMETHING MUCH BIGGER THAN YOUR SIMPLE MINDS CAN ENVISION.
IS THAT THE RADIOACTIVE MAN? I SAW HIM ON TV ONCE.
HE SOUNDS SMARTER THAN I REMEMBER--
HE'S A KILLER!
SSS
GHAAAAAAH!
YOU OKAY? YOU SHOULDN'T HAVE TRIED TO--
--I MEAN, I CAN FEEL US GETTING SUNBURNED ALL THE WAY OVER HERE--!
NOT ME! I'M FINE!
--NNNHHH--

I FLY THROUGH SPACE, DUDE! YOU KNOW HOW MUCH RADIATION THERE IS IN SPACE?
SHHHH...!
AW, MAN--!
HE REALLY HAS GOTTEN SMARTER! MY HELMET SAYS HE'S GONE ULTRAVIOLET, AND I DON'T THINK THERE'S A "SEE INVISIBLE STUFF" SETTING--!
THWIPP
THWIPP
THWIPP
THWIPP
SEE-THROUGH OR NOT, I BET HE'LL SHOW UP--
--IF I SPLORT OUT ALL THE WEBBING I'VE GOT AS ONE GIANT BLANKET!
I CAN EXPENSE THIS, RIGHT?
I MEAN, I'M AWARE WE DON'T HAVE STARK MONEY ANYMORE, BUT--
GUYS! THERE!
GET HIM!
GET HIM!

IT'S GOING DOWN!
BRACE YOURSELF FOR IMPACT AND THEN--
?
FAAASH
FWASH
THE ODDS WERE CERTAINLY NOT IN FAVOR OF THAT.
WHATEVER "THAT" MAY HAVE BEEN. HAVE WE ANY WORD FROM THE PUPS?
STEADY STATIC JUST NOW FADING. COME ON.

NOW.
I GAVE YOU *ONE ORDER*...
WHO? WHO DID THIS?

RADIOACTIVE MAN.
AND YOU LET HIM *ESCAPE*.
HEY, WE DIDN'T MEAN TO, BUT...
BUT *WHAT*, MILES?

GUYS! *THERE!*
GET HIM!

GET HIM!

...BUT A MAN WOULD HAVE DIED.

...
ONE MAN?
YES, SIR.
I SEE.
AND IN THE MOMENT YOU CHOSE TO LET THE ENEMY GO-- *IN THAT MOMENT*--DID *ANY* OF YOU STOP TO ASK YOURSELVES HOW MANY *MORE* LIVES YOU WERE PUTTING AT RISK?
NO?

GOOD. THEN WE RECRUITED WISELY. WELCOME TO THE TEAM.
YOU'RE-- NOT MAD--?
RADIOACTIVE MAN KILLED PEOPLE. WE WANTED TO AVENGE THEM, I SWEAR, BUT WE DIDN'T--
SIGH
LET ME STOP YOU RIGHT THERE. I TAKE THIS ESCAPE VERY, VERY SERIOUSLY, BUT BACK IN THE PLEISTOCENE ERA, WHEN WE CHOSE THE NAME "THE AVENGERS"--
--I DON'T EVEN REMEMBER WHO PICKED IT--
THE WASP.
--WHO STUCK AROUND FOR ABOUT A MONTH--IT WAS FROM THE HEAT OF BATTLE. PHILOSOPHICALLY, WE PROBABLY SHOULD HAVE GONE WITH "THE DEFENDERS" OR SOMESUCH.
BUT "AVENGERS" SOUNDS SO MUCH COOLER.
YOU'RE PREACHING TO THE CHOIR, SAM. OUR POINT IS, THE AVENGERS EXIST TO PROTECT PEOPLE. TO PRESERVE INNOCENT LIFE. THAT IS JOB ONE.
EVERYTHING ELSE--LIKE FIGURING OUT WHO UNLEASHED A DEPORTED CHINESE TERRORIST AND A MAGIC DRAGON ONTO A FEDERAL BANK--GETS PUT ON HOLD UNTIL--
PING
--NOW.
YOU GETTING A READING ON WHAT LIFTED THEM OUT?
SOME SORT OF TRANSTEMPORAL TELEPORTATION MATRIX...
...AND IT LOOKS LIKE A SIMILAR ONE IS OPENING UP ABOUT TEN BLOCKS SOUTH. LET'S GO SEE WHO ELSE WANTS TO COME OUT AND PLAY.
SOMEONE SEASONED WANT TO SAY IT THIS TIME?
AVENGERS ASSEMBLE!
NOT YOU.
SORRY.

#1 VARIANT BY **MAHMUD ASRAR** & **DAVE MCCAIG**

#1 VINTAGE VARIANT BY **ALEX ROSS**

#1 VARIANT BY **LUCIANO VECCHIO**

#1 HIP-HOP VARIANT
BY **JIM CHEUNG** & **JASON KEITH**

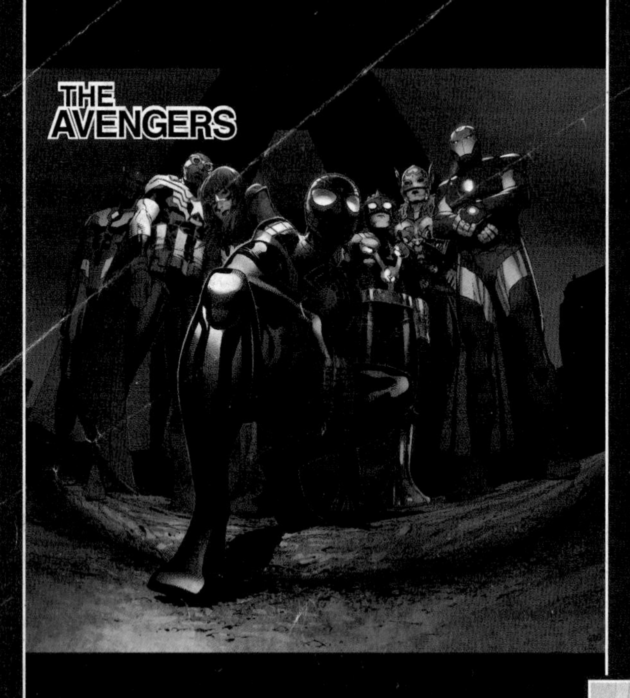

#1 INHUMANS 50TH ANNIVERSARY VARIANT
BY **CLIFF CHIANG**

#2 VARIANT
BY **OSCAR JIMENEZ**

#3 VARIANT
BY **AFU CHAN**

#3 VARIANT
BY **FRED HEMBECK** & **RACHELLE ROSENBERG**

#4 DEADPOOL VARIANT
BY **BOBBY RUBIO**